S0-FQJ-831

© **2010 by Rana Dirani**

All rights reserved. No part of this document may be reproduced or transmitted in any form or by any means, electronic, mechanical, photocopying, recording, or otherwise, without prior written permission of the author.

1st Edition 2010

ISBN 978-9953-0-1550-7

Published by Saifi Institute for Arabic Language, Beirut – Lebanon
+961 1 560738
Saifiarabic.com

Written by: Rana Dirani
Edited by: Mac McClenahan
Illustrated and designed by: Saro Ajemian & Roman Khorev - ORASWAY Multidisciplinary Design Studio

# SAIFI INSTITUTE FOR ARABIC LANGUAGE

Saifi Institute for Arabic Language aims to teach each student the practical skills he or she needs to communicate effectively and engagingly in Arabic. Since it was founded in 2007, in the Saifi district of Beirut near Martyr's Square, Saifi has become the largest Arabic language school in Lebanon, offering classes and exchange programs year round.

However, Saifi is more than just a language school; it is a linguistic institute dedicated to the study and teaching of both Lebanese and Classical (Modern Standard) Arabic. Saifi teachers are involved in developing the complete grammar and orthography (writing system) for the language spoken by Lebanese and their Syrian cousins – the first of its kind! In other words, Saifi teachers are not just teaching their native language, they are defining the nature of Lebanese Arabic, and developing innovative ways to teach it to others. Methods are embodied in the "Urban Arabic" series of textbooks, and also include cooking, video and ne

Students at Saifi come to learn how to communicate effectively with Lebanese (and Arabs in general given that the Lebanese dialect is widely understood), and some also come to learn Classical Arabic for academic reasons. They come from all walks of life: travelers, diplomats, students, NGO workers, and people raising their families in Lebanon. Hundreds of students from countries all around the word, including a large number of Lebanese who want to gain more understandings of the inner workings of their own language, have learned at Saifi.

# CONTENTS

# INTRODUCTION

This course is based on years of experience teaching students from around the world the *Beiruti* dialect of spoken Syrian Arabic. These students are the inspiration for *Urban 3arabic*. Their questions often lead to new insights and teaching methods, and their persistent desire to engage in effective and meaningful conversation with native speakers has led us to develop this curriculum, the aim of which is to impart both the practical skills and grammatical depth necessary to communicate in Arabic.

"Arabic is not an easy language to learn, but Rana's method, and this book, somehow makes it seem possible -- and fun. I wouldn't learn the language any other way."

-Josh Hersh, Journalist and former student

### What is Urban Arabic?

Urban Arabic is the culturally dominant mother tongue spoken in rapidly growing cities of the Arabic world and emulated throughout the countryside. It is the language of daily life, family life, love, and most Arab culture including music, TV shows and movies. Four major types of Urban Arabic are spoken in the Arab world: Maghrebi (Casablanca, Fez, Algiers), Egyptian (Cairo, Alexandria), Syrian (Damascus, Aleppo, Beirut, Amman, Jerusalem) and Gulf (Riyadh, Jeddah, Dubai, Kuwait).

Urban Arabic has no official orthography (writing system), and most Arabs learn to read and write in primary school using Modern Standard Arabic (MSA), the official language of Arab countries. The vastly different grammars, phonologies (pronunciations) and vocabularies of MSA and the four varieties Urban Arabic, which have more in common with each other than they do with MSA, mean that two unique, but not separate, languages are used in every Arab society.

This is not a modern development, however. Urban Arabic vernaculars have existed alongside Classical Arabic throughout the Middle East and North Africa since the spread of Islam from the Arabian Peninsula in the 7th and 8th centuries. Historically, Urban Arabic was called "Sedentary Arabic" (عربي حضري), because it was associated with settled Arabs, as opposed to nomadic Bedouins whose spoken language is closer to Classical Arabic.

The widespread use of Urban Arabic has been discussed, debated and denounced for hundreds of years, but the fact remains that it is the de facto mother tongue of the Arab world, passed on by parents to their children. Its influence is evident in Arabic poetry, modern popular culture, and the "mistakes" consistently found in classical and contemporary texts.

## Why Beiruti Urban Arabic?

Arab popular culture, perhaps more so than history, politics or religion, unites the entire Arab world from Morocco to Qatar. And, its stars, the singers, actors and televangelists, speak the language of the street: Urban Arabic. This curriculum teaches the Beiruti dialect of the Syrian variety of Urban Arabic, which, due to the cultural profligacy the Lebanese – well known for their TV shows, poetry and music – is one of the most widely understood of the Urban Arabic dialects, second only to Egyptian.

The diglossic reality (simultaneous use of two separate languages used for spoken and written communication) of the Arab world creates a dilemma for some beginning students who often ask the question: "Which type of Arabic should I study?" If your objective is to study Arabic/Islamic literature and history or speak at official events, you should study MSA. However, if your objective is to communicate with Arab people you should study Urban Arabic.

## Course progression

The Urban 3arabic curriculum begins by teaching the basics of survival in Lebanon, the foundations of spoken Arabic grammar, and the classical and "chatting" Arabic alphabet. Students then continue to expand their vocabulary and understanding of spoken Arabic syntax in order to become more comfortable and flexible communicating in social situations. Slowly the student is introduced to basic written Arabic material found in daily life and working situations. The course then moves on to the grammatical and lexical links between spoken and classical Arabic. Students learn to apply their knowledge to reading and w
ized and unfamiliar topics.

Upon completion of the complete the Urban 3arabic curriculum (Books 1 through 5) the student will be equipped with the skills to communicate in an effective and engaging manner in the same way that Arabs communicate among themselves; free from the rigidity of classical Arabic, yet more flexible and dynamic than local Arabic dialects.

## Goals: Book 1

This is an introductory book intended to be taken alongside Alif Baa: Introduction to Arabic Letters and Sounds (Brustad et al. 2006). Approximately 60 hours of class time, in addition to an equivalent amount of individual study and practice, are required to gain the basic survival proficiency taught in this book. Upon completing Urban Arabic Book 1 the student will gain the following skills:
- Proficiency in common courtesies used in daily life and formal situations
- Ability to ask about things and people and describe and understand their location
- Ability to conjugate verbs in the present tense
- Capacity to read and write names and pronounce new words written in the Arabic script.

## References

The Syntax of Spoken Arabic: A Comparative Study of Moroccan, Egyptian, Syrian and Kuwaiti Dialects, Brustad 2000; A Reference Grammar of Syrian Arabic, Cowell 2005; A Dictionary of Syrian Arabic: English-Arabic, Stowasser 2004.

# The Arabic Alphabet Reference Chart

| End | Middle | Beginning | Alone | Pronunciation / Chatting | | Example |
|-----|--------|-----------|-------|--------------|---------|---------|
| ـا | ـا | أ | ا | A | Arb3ah | Four |
| ـب | ـبـ | بـ | ب | B | Bayt | House |
| ـت | ـتـ | تـ | ت | T | Takhit | Bed |
| ـث | ـثـ | ثـ | ث | T/S | Massal | Example |
| ـج | ـجـ | جـ | ج | J/G | Jabal | Mountain |
| ـح | ـحـ | حـ | ح | H/7 | 7aram | Forbidden |
| ـخ | ـخـ | خـ | خ | Kh | Khalas | Enough |
| ـد | ـد | د | د | D | Djaj | Chicken |
| ـذ | ـذ | ذ | ذ | Z/D | Isstaz | Teacher |
| ـر | ـر | ر | ر | R | Riz | Rice |
| ـز | ـز | ز | ز | Z | Za3tar | Thyme |
| ـس | ـسـ | سـ | س | S | Siyarah | Car |
| ـش | ـشـ | شـ | ش | Sh | Showb | Hot weather |
| ـص | ـصـ | صـ | ص | S | Saff | Class |
| ـض | ـضـ | ضـ | ض | D | Da7yeh | Suburb |
| ـط | ـطـ | طـ | ط | T | Tabe2 | Floor |
| ـظ | ـظـ | ظـ | ظ | Z/D | Dohor | Noon |
| ـع | ـعـ | عـ | ع | AA/3 | 3arabi | Arabic |
| ـغ | ـغـ | غـ | غ | Gh | Ghali | Expensive |
| ـف | ـفـ | فـ | ف | F | Farid | Homework |
| ـق | ـقـ | قـ | ق | Q/2 | D2ee2ah | Minute |
| ـك | ـكـ | كـ | ك | K | Ka3ik | Special Lebanese bread |
| ـل | ـلـ | لـ | ل | L | Labneh | Labneh |
| ـم | ـمـ | مـ | م | M | Man2ousheh | Lebanese pizza |
| ـن | ـنـ | نـ | ن | N | Na3na3 | Mint |
| ـه/ه | ـهـ | هـ | ه | H | Hown | Here |
| ـو | ـو | و | و | W | Wa7ad | One |
| ـي | ـيـ | يـ | ي | Y | Yowm | Day |

The three letters that are marked with red above, have two functions: a consonant or a long vowel.

## Information about the Arabic script

1- Arabic is written from right to left.

2- All letters connect from right hand side, but not all connect to the left hand side.

3- The shapes of letters change, depending where the letter is located according to the chart above.

4- All Arabic words contain consonants and short vowels.

5- Every letter in any word, takes one short vowel or "sokoun". Usually these aren't written, but they're still there.

## Arabic Diacritical Symbols Reference Chart

| Short vowels | Kassrah | كسرة | ـِ |
| | Dammeh | ضمّة | ـُ |
| | Fat7ah | فتحة | ـَ |
| **Pronunciation symbols** | Sokoun | سكون | ْ |
| | Shaddeh | شدّة | ّ |
| | Alif maddeh | ألف مدّة | آ |
| | Hamzeh | همزة | ء |
| **Grammatical symbols** | Alif maqssoura | ألف مقصورة | ى |
| | Ta-marboutah | تاء مربوطة | ـة / ة |

## The definite article ("the")

The definite article in Arabic is a prefix , and is written as "Al" ( الـ ). The *pronunciation* of the definite article depends on whether the word is starting with Moon or Sun letter.

| ي | و | ه | م | ك | ق | ف | غ | ع | خ | ح | ج | ب | أ | 🌙 |
|---|---|---|---|---|---|---|---|---|---|---|---|---|---|---|
| Y | W | H | M | K | Q/2 | F | GH | 3 | KH | 7 | J | B | A | |

"moon letter": if a word is starting with a moon, the definite article "L" keeps its sound.

Ex: ktab >> lktab                     كتاب << الكتاب

| ن | ل | ظ | ط | ض | ص | ش | س | ز | ر | ذ | د | ث | ت | ☀️ |
|---|---|---|---|---|---|---|---|---|---|---|---|---|---|---|
| N | L | Z/D | T | D | S | SH | S | Z | R | Z/D | D | S/T | T | |

"sun letter": if a word is starting with a sun letter, don't pronouce the "L" and the pronounciation of the first letter should be emphasized by adding the shadda (ّ).

Ex: siyarah >> ssiyarah                     سيارة << السّيارة

## Hint

Say each letters out loud and notice how the pronunciation of the moon letters comes from the back of your mouth, while the sun letters come from the front (your teeth). If you can learn to associate this difference with the definite article it makes learning the sun and moon letters easier.

# KEY TO CHATTING ALPHABET (PHONETICS)

The Arabic chatting alphabet or Arabesh ("Arabizi" or "عربيزي") is used to communicate in the Arabic language over the Internet or for sending messages via cellular phones. Users of this alphabet have developed some special notations to transliterate Arabic sounds that do not exist in the Latin alphabet. We have decided to use this system as a bridge for to learning the Arabic script because of it is increasignly used by Arab youth.

During the last few decades and especially since the 1990s, Western-invented text communication technologies have become increasingly prevalent in the Arab world, such as personal computers, the internet, email, instant messaging and mobile phone text messaging. Most of these technologies originally had the ability to communicate using the Latin alphabet only, and some of them still do not have the Arabic alphabet as an optional feature, often times with limited functionality. As a result, Arabic speaking users communicated in these technologies by transliterating the Arabic text into the Latin

lent in the Latin script, numerals and other characters were appropriated. For example, the numeral "3" is used to represent the Arabic letter "ع" ("ayn").

| Chatting letter | Arabic equivalent | Explanation |
|---|---|---|
| 7 | ح | This letter is pronounced like a deep English 'h'. The air comes from your stomach and your throat should be tightened. We make this sound when we blow steam out of our mouths; to clean glasses for instance. Ex: "How" uses this deep 'h' sound; it would be spelled "7ow" using the Arabic chatting alphabet. |
| 2 | ق، ء | This letter signifies a 'guttural stop'. An abrupt stop in the sound of a word. It is the sound you make when you are punched in the stomach, and in the middle of the word "UH-OH!". |
| 3 | ع | Imagine the sound you make when the destist or doctor tells you to "say aaaa". The 'aa' sound is what this letter signifies. Ex: "al-Qaaida" uses this long 'aa' sound; it would be spelled "al-Qa3ida" using the Arabic chatting alphabet. |
| Gh | غ | Gargle, and this is the sound that you make. Vibrate your tonsils by tightening your throat and breathing out. Ex: "Baghdad" and "Abu Ghraib" both have the 'gh' sound. |
| Kh | خ | This sound is similar to gh, but higher up; it comes from your mouth more than your throat. It is the sound you make in preparing to clear your throat or 'hock a luggi'. Ex: The German word "nacht" would be spelled "nakht" using the Arabic chatting alphabet. |

## A: SAYING HELLO AND GETTING TO KNOW SOMEONE

### Greeting

| Hi / hello | Mar7aba | مرحَبا |
| Peace be upon you | Assalamu 3alaykom | السَّلام عليكم |

### Reply

| Welcome (hi) | Ahlein | أهلِين |
| Welcome (hi) | Ahlan wa sahlan | أهلاً و سـهلاً |
| "Two hellos" | Mar7abtein | مرحبتين |
| And on you the same | Wa 3alaykom assalam | وعليكم السلام |

AHLEIN أهلين

Now you know why Arabs always say "welcome" when replying to "hi."

# LANGUAGE PRACTICE

Fill in the balloons with the greetings that correspond to the different situations.

A -

B -

A -

B -

A -

B -

# LANGUAGE DISCOVERY

There is special greeting that people use in taxis and when people are working. Find it, and write it down.

A- Rakib (passenger): ya3tik...

B-Chauffeur taxi (taxi driver):

TAXI

$3245  ٣٣٤٥ ص

# LANGUAGE CULTURE

Try the greetings we have learned and listen carefully to the replies that people use. What are the different greeting styles used around Beirut (EXTRA: are there differences according to the age of the speaker)?

Hamra

Da7yeh

Achrafieh

Jabal

## B: "HOW?" & "WHAT?"

Question words (interrogatives) in Arabic always come at the beginning of the sentence.

**HOW?**
How are you (m-f-pl)?
How's your health (m)?
How's it going?
**WHAT?**
What's your news (f)?

KEEF?
Keefak/ keefik/ keefkon?
Keef sa7tak?
Keef l7al?
SHOU?
Shou akhbarik?

كيف؟
كيفَك / كيفِك / كيفكُن؟
كيف صحتَك ؟
كيف الحَال؟
شـو؟
شـو أخبارِك ؟

# QUESTIONS

# ANSWERS

Good, fine (m-f-pl)
Very good (m)
Praise god
Everything is perfect
Everything is fine
Nothing new
"So-so", I mean...

Mnee7/ mnee7a/ mnai7
Kteer mnee7
L7amdilla
Kill shi tamam
Mashi l7al
Ma shi jdeed
Ya3ni

منيح / منيحة / مناح
كتير منيح
الحمدلله
كل شي تمام
ماشي الحال
ما شـي جديد
يعني

**Note:** These answers can be used interchangeably with the given questions. You can mix-and-match, as long it makes a good combination (ask for the help of your teacher).

And...
You (m-f-pl)

Wo or wa
Inta - Inti - Intou

و
إنتَ - إنتِ - إنتو

# LANGUAGE PRACTICE

Using the pictures as a guide, write the appropriate conversations.
Try to add words that people use to address each other when they greet.
Ex: "mister", "beauty", "dear" etc. (ask your teacher).

A -

B -

A -

B -

A -

B -

A -

B -

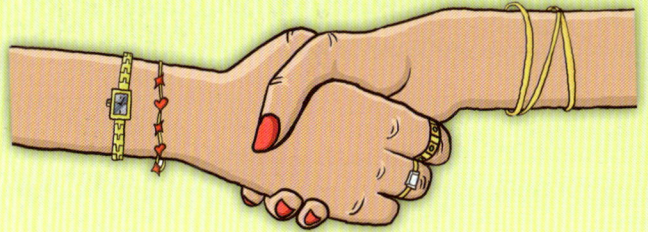

A -

B -

A -

B -

## C: ASKING ABOUT NAMES...

What's your (m-f) name?
My name is...
Nice to meet you

Shou issmak/ issmik?
Issmi....
Tcharrafna

شـو إسـمَك / إسـمِك؟
إسـمي.....
تشرّفنا

## Exercise 1.C:
# LANGUAGE PRACTICE

Choose one of your classmates, greet them, introduce yourself, and ask how they are doing. Write your conversation below:

A -

A -

A -

A -

B -

B -

B -

B -

**Note:** As we mentioned before, you can use greetings and replies interchangeably. You can even repeat the greeting-reply exchange. The more you use these expressions the more you prove that you aren't afraid of using the language. It makes the other person who's speaking with you feel comfortable and helps keep the conversation going.

**Different ways to bid farewell**

- Do you (m) need anything before I leave?
- No, have a safe trip. (as thanks for asking)

- Baddak shi?
- La, ma3 salameh

- بدّك شي؟
- لأ مع السّلامة

- Have a safe trip (say when someone is leaving you)
- God bless you (m)

- Ma3 salameh
- Allah yssalmak

- مع السلامة
- الله يسلمَك

- Excuse me
- You (m) are excused

- Bil2izin
- Iznak ma3ak

- بالإذن
- إذنَك معَك

- May god reward you (m) with good health
- May god reward you (m) too

- Ya3tik l3afyeh
- Allah y3afik.

- يعطيك العافية
- الله يعافيك

The main word in the next conversations is "Yalla"

YALLA!

**Note:** The meaning of "yalla" varies from one conversation to another. The most basic meanings are: "let's go", or "hurry up". As you listen and practice you will learn many other ways to use perhaps the most commonly spoken word in the Arab world, "yalla"!

# Informal ways to say "good bye"

- Yalla bye

- Bye Samir.

- Yalla bye Jad.

- Ma3 salameh bye.

- Yalla bye Jad.
- Allah yssalmak bye.

- Ma3 salameh Samir.
- Bye.

- La ma3 salameh Samir.
- Bye.

- Yalla bye Jad, Baddak shi?
- Allah yssalmak bye.

يلّا باي!

Samir

Jad

# Formal ways to say "good bye"

- Yalla bil2izin!
- Allah yssalmak, bye.

- Iznak ma3ak, ma3 salameh.
- Bye.

- Yalla bil izin, ya3tik l3afyeh.

- Iznak ma3ak, ma3 salameh.

# LANGUAGE PRACTICE

Read the following conversations and fill in the blanks with the appropriate word.

- Mar7aba Diala.
- Mnee7a _____ , wo inti?
- Ma shi _____. Keef _____?
- Yalla _____shi?

- Ahlein Rita, _____?
- Mashi l7al, tamam. Shou _____?
- _____ , l7amdillah.
- La ma3 _____

— Rita    Diala →

- Mar7aba, _____ l3afyeh isstaz Hamid.
- _____ , l7amdillah wo inta?
- Iznak ma3ak isstaz. Ma3 _____

- Ahlein, allah y3afik Marwan. Keefak, mnee7?!
- l7amdillah, tamam. Yalla _____
Marwan.
- Allah _____ , bye.

Marwan

Isstaz Hamid →

## Lesson review
After finishing this lesson and practicing inside and outside the class you should be able to:
- Greet people using casual and formal expressions
- Meet people and introduce yourself
- Say "goodbye" by using casual as well as polite expressions

# LESSON 2
## THIS IS MINE, THANK YOU

## A: DEMONSTRATIVES: "This is Arabic!"

All Arabic nouns and demonstratives (this, that etc.) are either feminine or masculine, and the easiest way to know the difference is by learning to recognize the "Ta-marboutah" (ة).
- Ta-marboutah (ة) is the feminine symbol, and comes ONLY at the end of feminine nouns.  It is pronounced as either "ah" or "eh".
- Be careful, not all feminine nouns have  Ta-marboutah!!

| | | |
|---|---|---|
| This (m) | Hayda | هيدا |
| This (f) | Haydi | هيدي |
| These (pl) | Haydol | هيدول |
| Those** | Haydak | هيداك |
| That (m)** | Haydik | هيديك |
| That (f)** | Haydoleek | هيدوليك |
| No | La | لا |
| Not + (nouns & adj) | Mish | مش |
| Yes | Eh* | إي* |
| Who is? | Meen? | مين؟ |
| Whose is? | Lameen? | لمين؟ |
| To | La____ | لــ |

* "Eh" is also used to emphasize a negative answer
    Ex: "This is not your pen?" can be answered either "no" (la) or, with more emphasis, "yes, it isn't my pen", "eh, hayda mish alami"

** "Hayda", "haydi" and "haydol" have a broad meaning and are often used in place of these words.

# Exercise 1.A:
## LANGUAGE PRACTICE

Answer the following questions about these people.

**TONY**

ex: - Hayda Marwan?
- La hayda mish Marwan, hayda Tony.

HAMID    DIALA    GEORGES    NOURA    ALINE    BOB    RITA    MOUSTAPHA

Hayda TONY?        Haydi DIALA?        Meen hayda?        Hayda mish BOB?

_____        _____        _____        _____

_____        _____        _____        _____

Haydi DIALA?        Meen haydi?        Haydi NOURA?        Hayda BOB?

_____        _____        _____        _____

_____        _____        _____        _____

Meen Feiruz? Ask your friends and write a short description (in English).

## Masculine nouns:

**Hayda bayt**
هيدا بيت

**Hayda alam**
هيدا قلم

**Hayda maktab**
هيدا مكتب

**Hayda ktab**
هيدا كتاب

**Hayda daftar**
هيدا دفتر

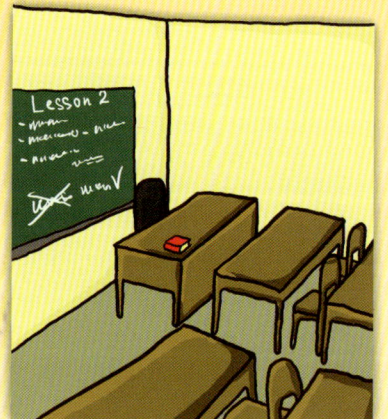

**Hayda saff**
هيدا صف

**Hayda isstaz**
هيدا إستاذ

**Hayda finjan**
هيدا فنجان

**Hayda shoghol**
هيدا شغل

## Exercise 3.A:
# LANGUAGE PRACTICE

Practice your detective skills (and vocabulary) by answering the questions below.

**Shou hayda?**

**Shou hayda?**

**Shou hayda?**

**Shou hayda?**

**Shou hayda?**

**Shou haydi?**

## Feminine nouns:

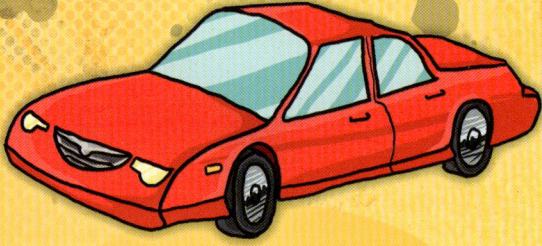

**Haydi siyarah**
هيدي سيارة

**Haydi kibbayeh**
هيدي كبّاية

**Haydi jareedeh**
هيدي جريدة

**Haydi tawleh**
هيدي طاولة

**Haydi arid**
هيدي أرض

**Haydi shajrah**
هيدي شجرة

**Haydi shantah**
هيدي شنتة

**Haydi m3almeh**
هيدي معلمة

**Haydi sa3ah**
هيدي ساعة

Find out the meanings of the following words by asking friends, and categorize them as either masculine or feminine.

**Hint:** Use this expression to find the meaning of English words in Arabic: "shou ya3ni ____ bil 3arabi?" ("what's the meaning of ____ in Arabic?")

تخت - برنامج - محمة؟ - سهرة - اجتماع - مقابلة - قهوة - مطعم

Bed – schedule – traffic – party – meeting – interview – coffee – restaurant.

| Masculine | Feminine |
|---|---|
| _____ | _____ |
| _____ | _____ |
| _____ | _____ |
| _____ | _____ |

## B: PRONOUNS

In Arabic there are two pronoun forms, and each form has particular uses. The chart below lists all the uses of Arabic pronouns. We will learn these throughout the rest of this book.

| | English pronouns | Pronoun Suffixes | | Independent Pronouns | |
|---|---|---|---|---|---|
| | English pronouns each have a different function: subject, object or possession | SUBJECT OBJECT POSSESSION | | Independent pronouns function only as subject. | |
| | | Suffix pronouns have three functions: subject, object and possession. | | | |
| **1st Person** | I me my | ___ i (ni) | ـــ ي (ني) | Ana | أنا |
| - Plural | we us our | ___ na | ـــ نا | Ni7na | نِحنا |
| | | | | | |
| **2nd Person** | | | | | |
| - Masculine | you your | ___ ak | ـــَ ك | Inta | إنتَ |
| - Feminine | you your | ___ ik/ki | ـِ ك /كي | Inti | إنتِ |
| - Plural | you your | ___ kon | ـــ كُن | Intou | إنتو |
| | | | | | *You guys* |
| **3rd Person** | | | | | |
| - Masculine | he him it (m) his its (m) | ___ oh | ـــ ـُه | Huwwe | هوّ |
| - Feminine | she her it (f) hers its (f) | ___ ha/a | ـــ ها/ا | Hiyye | هيّ |
| - Plural | they them their (pl) | ___ on/hon | ـــُن /هُن | Hinne | هنّ |

As we learned with the Arabic demonstratives (that, this etc.) all singular nouns are either feminine or masculine. The same is also true of pronouns, hence, the gender neutral pronoun "it" does not exist in Arabic. Can you figure out which six Arabic pronoun forms correspond to "it/its"?

1) _____   2) _____ 3) _____

4) _____ 5) _____ 6) _____

Huwwe Abou Ahmad

Hiyye Haifa

Using the pronoun table match the words in the left column, which have the possessive pronoun suffix, with the independent pronouns in the right column.

Ktaboh •
Alamon •
Shoghola •
Maktabkon •
M3almitna •
Issmak •
Siyarti •
Isstazik •

• Hiyye
• Intou
• Ana
• Huwwe
• Inti
• Hinne
• Inta
• Ni7na

Indicating possession in Arabic can be done in three ways:

1) Pronoun suffix
2) Possessive pronoun (page 28)
3) Genitive construction (page 32)

SUBJECT    OBJECT    POSSESSION

## 1) Possessive suffixes:

Examples:
(Can you tell which noun is feminine?)

| | Suffix | | M3almeh | Shoghol |
|---|---|---|---|---|
| My | ___ i | ___ ي | M3almti | Shogholi |
| Your (m) | ___ ak | ___َ ك | M3almtak | Shogholak |
| Your (f) | ___ ik | ___ ِك | M3almtik | Shogholik |
| His | ___ oh | ___ ُه | M3almtoh | Shogholoh |
| Her | ___ ha/a | ___ها/ا | M3almita* | Shoghola |
| Our | ___ na | ___ نا | M3almitna* | Shogholna |
| Your (pl) | ___ kon | ___ كُن | M3almitkon* | Shogholkon |
| Their | __hon/on | __هُن/ُن | M3almiton* | Shogholon |

* "Ta-marboutah" (ة) is the symbol of feminine, and it always changes to be "T" (ت) when it's followed by a suffix.

# LANGUAGE PRACTICE

Translate the following sentences to Arabic practicing possessive suffixes.

This is my cup.

This is his note book.

This is her bag.

This is our teacher (f).

Is this your (m) house?

This is their teacher (m).

Is this your (f) ground?

Is this your (pl) newspaper?

This is his table.

This is my car.

This is her watch.

Is this his mug?

This is your (m) bag.

Is this your (f) bag?

Put the words in the watermelon into the columns corresponding to their possesive suffix.

| His | Their | Your (pl) | Our | Her | My |
| --- | --- | --- | --- | --- | --- |
| | | | | | |
| | | | | | |
| | | | | | |

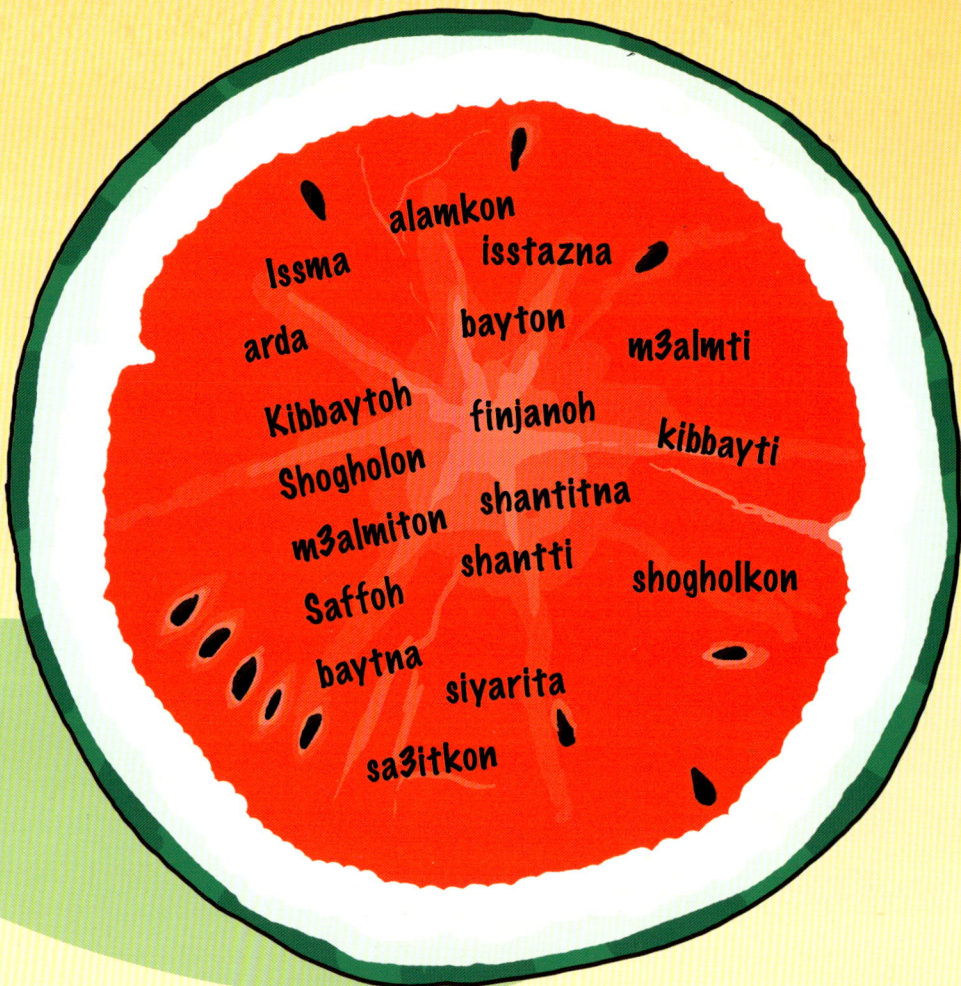

alamkon

Issma    isstazna

bayton

arda    m3almti

Kibbaytoh    finjanoh

kibbayti

Shogholon

m3almiton    shantitna

shantti

Saffoh    shogholkon

baytna

siyarita

sa3itkon

# 2 ) Possessive pronouns

Possessive pronouns come directly AFTER the object being possessed.
Ex: "Daftar eloh", "Hayda elak?"

Mine    El**i**    إل**ي**

Yours(m)    El**ak**    إل**َك**

Yours(f)    El**ik**    إل**ِك**

His    El**oh**    إل**ُه**

Hers    El**a**    إل**ا**

Ours    El**na**    إل**نا**

Yours(pl)    El**kon**    إل**كُن**

Theirs    El**on**    إل**نُ**

Note: Eli, elak, etc. comes from the preposition "la___" (ل___), which means "To____". When an object is attached to the preposition "la" using the pronoun suffix it becomes a prepositional phrase and gains a flexible meaning close to "to me" = "mine", "to you" = "yours" etc...

# LANGUAGE PRACTICE

Read the following sentences and create another sentence that expresses the same meaning in a different way.

Ex: This is my book >>> This is mine.

| | |
|---|---|
| **Haydi siyarah elna.** <br> هيدي السيارة إلنا | هيدي سيارتنا |
| **Hayda lmaktab eloh.** <br> هيدا المكتب إلهُ | هيدا مكتبه |
| **Hayda ktabi.** <br> هيدا كتابي | هيدا إلي |
| **Hayda lbayt elkon.** <br> هيدا البيت إلكُن | هيدا بيتكن |
| **Haydi kirssitna.** <br> هيدي كرسِتنا | هيدي النا |
| **Hayda finjanon.** <br> هيدا فنجانن | هيدا إلنا |
| **Haydi kibbayti.** <br> هيدي كبّايتي | هيدي إلي |

Haydi eli !
3aw!! 3aw!!

# Exercise 4.C:
## LANGUAGE PRACTICE

Write the questions for the following answers, using all the different ways you have learned to express possession.

| | |
|---|---|
| هل هيدا اكتابك؟ | La, hayda liktab mish eli, hayda eloh.<br>لا.هيدا الكتاب مش إلي، هيدا إلَه. |
| هيدا بيتكن؟ | Eh, hayda lbayt elna.<br>إي. هيدا البيت إلنا. |
| لمين هيدي السيارة؟ | Yimkin haydi siyarah ela. _(perhaps)_<br>يمكِن هيدي السّيارة إلا . |
| هيدي الجريدة إلن؟ | La, haydi ljareedeh mish elon, haydi eli.<br>لا. هيدي الجريدة مش إلّن. هيدي إلي. |
| لمين هيدي الكبّاية؟ | Ma ba3rif lameen haydi lkibbayeh. _(know)_<br>ما بعرِف لمين هيدي الكبّاية. |
| هيدي معلّمتكن؟ | La, haydi mish m3almitna.<br>لا. هيدي مش معلمتنا. |
| هيدا استاذكن؟ | La, yimkin hayda isstazon.<br>لا. يمكن هيدا إستاذُن. |
| هيدا الدفتر مش إلَه؟ | Eh, daftar mish eloh.<br>إي. الدّفتر مش إلَه. |
| هيدي سيارتن؟ | La, akeed mish siyariton.<br>لا. أكيد مش سيارتُن. |
| هيدي أرضه؟ | La, haydi l2arid elna.<br>لا. هيدي الأرض إلنا. |
| هيدي سيارة راهم؟ | La, yimkin haydi siyarit Ibrahim.<br>لا. يمكِن هيدي سيارة إبراهيم . |
| لمين هيدول القلم والدّفتر؟ | Ma ba3rif, mish eli haydol l2alam w daftar.<br>ما بعرِف. مش إلي هيدول القلَم والدّفتر. |
| هيدا اكتابه؟ | La, hayda mish ktaboh.<br>لا. هيدا مش كتابُه. |
| لمين هيدول كتاب وشنتة؟ | Haydol ktab w shantit Joumana.<br>هيدول كتاب وشنتة جمانة. |

**Extra vocabulary:**

| | | |
|---|---|---|
| Maybe, perhaps | Yimkin | يمكِن |
| I don't know | Ma ba3rif | ما بعرف |
| Of course, for sure, definitely | Akeed | أكيد |

30

Circle the word in each list that doesn't fit (gender, possession, etc.).

| | | | | |
|---|---|---|---|---|
| m3almita | ardon | (saffoh) | tawlitna | kibbayti |
| baytna | ktabna | daftarna | shogholna | (isstaza) |
| kibbayita | siyarita | (finjana) | jareedita | |
| (Elik) | saffak | alamak | keefak | issmak |
| Saffon | keefkon | haydol | (hayda) | |

ma3 salameh!

## Lesson Review
After finishing this lesson and practicing inside and outside the class you should be able to:
- Ask about objects and possession using demonstratives (this, that, etc.)
- Ask who people are and if something is theirs

# LESSON 3
## I WANT WHAT HE HAS

## A: GENITIVE CONSTRUCTION: "Bob's Friends"

Use two nouns in sequence to create the genitive construction. The first noun is possessed, and the second noun is the possessor.

### Tawlit   Im3almeh

Possessed -
Is defined by the possessor -
(i.e. it cannot have a definite article)
The ta-marboutah (ــة) "becomes "t" (ت)-

- Possessor
- Can have a definite article

## Vocabulary

| | | |
|---|---|---|
| Money | Massari | مَصاري |
| Change (of money) | Fratah (Srafeh) | فُراطَة (صُرافِة) |
| Friend (m - f - pl) | Sadee2/ Sadee2ah / Asdiqa2 | صَديق / صَديقَة / أصْدِقاءُ |
| Boyfriend – Girlfriend – Friends | Sa7ib / Sa7beh / As7ab | صاحِب / صاحْبِة / أصْحاب |
| Companion (m - f- pl) | Rfee2 / Rfee2ah / Rif2at | رُفيق / رُفيقَة / رِفُقات |

## Exercise 1.A:
## LANGUAGE PRACTICE

Use one word from each card to write four sentences.

| Hayda | Sa7ib | Shirine |
|---|---|---|
| Haydi | Rif2at | Kamal |
| Haydol | Massari | Marwan |
| | Sa7beh | Abbass |
| | Sadi2ah | Hiba |

Using genetive construction to indicate possession

Using pronoun suffix to indicate possession

إضافة

1:

1:

2:

2:

# B: PSEUDO VERBS: "Do you have what I want?"

SUBJECT   OBJECT   POSSESSION

The pronoun suffix is used to specify the subject when conjugating pseudo verbs in the imperfective (non-past) tense. Study the examples and fill in the rest of the table below.

(I can) خ

| to want Badd+ (pronoun suffix) ___+بدّ | | | to have 3ind + (pronoun suffix) ___+عِند | | | to have with ma3 + (pronoun suffix) ___+ مع | |
|---|---|---|---|---|---|---|---|
| I want | | بدي | I have | | عندي | Have with me | Ma3i |
| You(m) want | | بدّك | You(m) have | | | Have with you(m) | معَك |
| You (f) want | Baddik | | You(f) have | | | Have with you(f) | |
| He wants | | | He has | | عندُه | Has with him | Ma3oh |
| She wants | | | She has | | | Has with her | معا |
| We want. | | | We have | 3indna | | Have with us | |
| You(pl) want | | | You(pl) have | | عندكُن | Have with you(pl) | |
| They want | | بدّن | They have | | | Have with them | Ma3on |

**NOTE:** To negate any verb, use "ma" before it.
EX: "Ma baddi" = "I don't want",
"Ma 3indoh" = "He doesn't have"

# LANGUAGE DISCOVERY

1 - First find out the meaning of the following food words in singular and plural (you might have heard them or seen them on menus).
2 - Write three conversations based on the new words. Try to write the polite expressions that you might have heard, especially "tfadall", which is commonly used to mean "here you go" when giving something to someone.

منقوشة

عرنوس عرانيس؟
ليمون

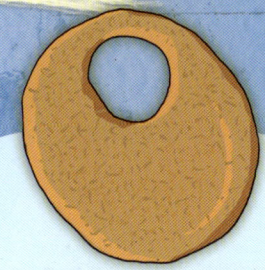

كعكة وكعك

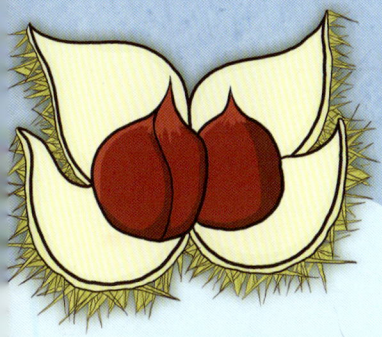

كستنا

كباية عصير

قنّينة مي

## Conversation 1

A – 3indak ka3ik?                    B – eh!

A – Baddi _____ w 3asseer.        B – _____

A – _____ اديني بدّي ريد          B – _____

## Conversation 2

A – _____        B – _____

A – _____        B – _____

A – _____        B – _____

## Conversation 3

A – _____        B – _____

A – _____        B – _____

A – _____        B – _____

# LANGUAGE PRACTICE

Let's practice helping verbs by translating the following sentences into Arabic.

**Extra vocabulary**

| | | |
|---|---|---|
| But, only, enough, just | Bass | بس |
| Now | Halla2 | هلأ |

ARGILEH?

1 – I have a book.  عندي كتاب

2 – He wants a cup of coffee  بده منجان قهوة

3 – What do you (f) want?  شو بدك

4 – What does she want?  شو بدها

5 – What do you (pl) have?  شو عندكن

6 – Do you have a house?  عندك بيت

7 – I have your (m) book but not her book  عندي كتابك بس مش كتابها

8 – I want coffee but not now!  بدي قهوة بس مش هلأ

9 – Do you (pl) have argileh?  عندكن أرجلة

10 – We want argileh tiffa7tein.  بدنا

11 – Do you(f) have a class now?  عندك صف هلأ

Write a sentence describing the following situations.

عندهن سيارة صفرا
yellow

لو بدا كعكة

لو عنده كتاب

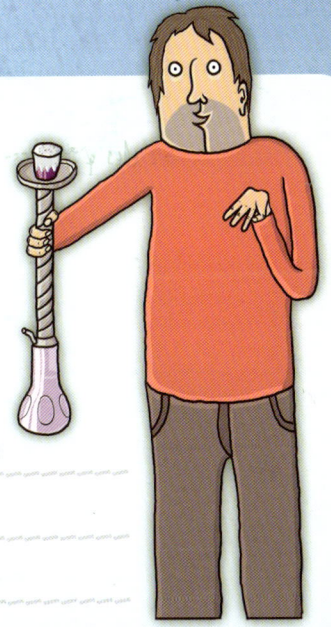

يدخّن أرجيلة (نفخّا)

## C: PREPOSITIONS & LOCATIONS

| Where? | Wein? | وين؟ |
|---|---|---|
| On/to | 3ala | على |
| To, or for (someone) | La | لـ |
| From | Min | مِن |
| In (there is, there are) | Fi | في |
| Above (over, up) | Fow2 | فوق |
| Under (below, down) | Ta7t | تحت |
| Next to (beside) | 7ad | حد |
| Behind | Wara | ورا |
| In front (across) | Eddam (biwij) | إدام (بوّج) |
| Between | Bayn | بَين |
| Here | Hown | هون |
| There | Honeek | هونيك |
| In / at | Bi | بـ |

**Note:** After a preposition always add the definite article to nouns, unless the nouns are also described as being possessed.
EX: 1) right: Ana 7ad lbayt; wrong: Ana 7ad bayt
  2) right: Ana 7ad bayt Rami (Ana 7ad baytoh);
    wrong: Ana 7ad lbayt Rami

**Extra:** These words and meanings cannot take a pronoun suffix.

# LANGUAGE PRACTICE

SUBJECT · OBJECT · POSSESSION

Finish adding pronoun suffixes to the following prepositions in order to create prepositional phrases

| 7ad | Wein? | Fow2 | Ta7t | Eddam | Fi |
|------|--------|-------|-------|--------|------|
| حد | وين؟ | فوق | تحت | إدام | في |
| حدّي | ~~وينيّ~~ | فوقي | تحتي | إدامي | فيّ |
| حدك | وينك | **فوقك** | تحتك | ادامك | فيك |
| حدك | وينك | فوقك | **تحتِك** | ادامك | فيكي/اك |
| خده | وينه | فوقه | تحته | **إدامُه** | فيه |
| حدها | وينها | فوقها | تحتها | ادامها | **فيها** |
| **حدُن** | وينهن | فوقهن | تحتهن | ادامهن | فيهن |
| حدكن | **وينكُن؟** | فوقكن | تحتكن | ادامكن | فيكن |
| حدنا | وينّا | فوقنا | **تحتنا** | ادامنا | فينا |

**Note:** "Bi" and "fi" mean the same thing when used in a prepositional phrase: "in (some container)". The difference is that "bi" NEVER accepts a pronoun suffix, while "fi" ALWAYS has a pronoun suffix attached. When the container is a first or second person noun (e.g. ana, inta, inti, intu) "fi" is always used.

# LANGUAGE PRACTICE

Fill in the blanks to make meaningful sentences.

1 - Ahmad _____ lmadrasseh.
- Bi
- Fi
- Wara

2 - Shoghloh _____ baytoh.
- 7ad
- Fow2
- Bi

3 - Ahlan wa sahlan _____ lebnan.
- 7ad
- 3ala
- Bi

4 - Baddi kibbayit birah _____ tawleh.
- 3a
- Ta7t
- Biwij

5 - Siyartoh mish _____ lbayt.
- Ta7t
- Bi
- Fow2

6 - Madrassti _____ bayti.
- Wara
- Ta7t
- 7adi

Answer the questions below, and figure out the definition of the new words from the picture or by asking your friends.

بسينة: ــــــــــــ
كلب: ــــــــــــ

وين البسينة؟
البسينة حد الكلِب

حيّة: ــــــــــــ

وين الحيّة؟
ــــــــــــ احات

وين زيزي؟
ــــــــــــ

جبنة: ــــــــــــ

وين الجبنة؟
ــــــــــــ

وين كريم؟

ــــــــــــــــــــ وراء ــــــــــــــــــــ

كنباية:

وين الكَلِب؟

ـــــــــــــــــــــــــــــــــــــــ

وين السيارة؟

ـــــــــــــــــــــــــــــــــــــــ

# LANGUAGE PRACTICE

Write one sentence for each picture describing the location of all the objects in relation to each other.

# LANGUAGE PRACTICE

Translate the following questions and answers between Ahmad and Zeina to Arabic:

Q - Do you have a house?

_____

Q - Where is my cup?

_____

Q - Does she have a car?

_____

Q - Where is our teacher (f)?

_____

Q - Where is his bag?

_____

Q - Where is your office?

_____

A - Yes it's in Hamra.

_____

A - It's on the table.

_____

A - Yes it's under her work in the parking lot.

_____

A - She's in the classroom in front of them.

_____

A - It's on the chair behind you.

_____

A - It's beside his office.

_____

AHMAD

ZEINA

## D: BEING POLITE

There are different ways to say "please" in Arabic, and especially in Lebanon. We will introduce them all but, you only need to choose one and make it yours.

Be ready for replies, it opens a door for you to speak in Arabic more. It's not enough to say just one part of the conversation.

This is a literal translation of a Lebanese conversation using please:

Hi, may god reward you.

Please, I want............

Thanks a lot, you are full of manners.

Excuse me, do you need anything?

God bless you, bye

Welcome, may god reward you too.

You are welcome. Go ahead, here is what you asked for.

Welcome, walaw.

No, go with peace.

Bye.

**Extra vocabulary:**
no worries, it's a pleasure = Walaw  وَلَو

# Vocabulary related to "please"

Below are literal translations of different ways to say "please" and several replies.
As usual, you can mix and match!

*like way I...?*
*few more*

| | | |
|---|---|---|
| Do me a favor (m / f / pl) | 3mol/ 3meli / 3melou ma3rouf... | ...عمول / عملي / عملو معروف |
| If you (m / f / pl) permit | Law sama7t/ sama7ti/ sama7tou... | ...لو سمحت / سمحتي / سمحتو |
| If you accept (m / f / pl) | Iza bitreed/ bitreedi/ bitreedou... | إذا بتريد / بتريدي / بتريدو... |
| Of your generosity (m / f / pl) | Min fadlak/ fadlik/ fadlkon... | من فضلَك / فضلِك / فضلكُن... |
| Sorry | 3afwan | عفواً |

## Ways to say "please"

## Replies

| | | |
|---|---|---|
| Thanks | Shukran | شـكـراً |
| Thanks (Less formal) | yisslamou | يِسلَمو |
| You (m / f / pl) are full of manners | Killak / killik / kilkon zow2 | كلَّك / كلِّك / كلكُن ذوق |
| You (m / f / pl) are welcome | Tikram / tikrami / tikramou | تِكرَم / تكرَمي / تكرَمو |
| Go ahead (m / f / pl) | Tfaddall / tfaddali / tfaddalou | تفضّل / تفضّلي / تفضّلو |

# ...NGUAGE PRACTICE

Write two conversations in different situations using your new vocabulary.
Ask your teacher or your friends for more words if you need them.

## Extra vocabulary that you might need in your conversation:

| | | |
|---|---|---|
| I get out (of the car/bus) here | Binzal hown | .بنزّل هون |
| The bill | Li7ssab | الحساب |

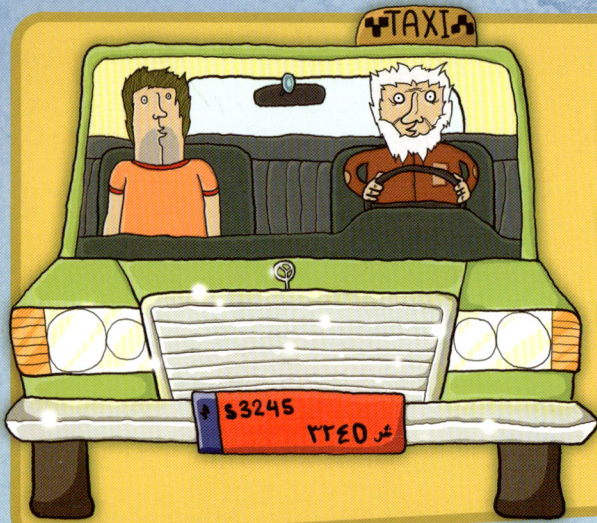

| You | Taxi Driver |
|---|---|
| | |
| | |
| | |
| | |

| You | Waiter at a "snack" * |
|---|---|
| | |
| | |
| | |
| | |

\* "Snack" is often used in Lebanon to refer to a Lebanese fast-food restaurant.

### Lesson Review
After finishing this lesson and practicing inside and outside the class you should be able to:
- Ask and answer questions about wants, ownership & locations
- Indicate the location of objects in relation to other objects using prepositions
- Use courtesies like please and thank you

# LESSON 4
## " I AM A STUDENT LEARNING ARABIC! "

## A: IMPERFECTIVE* VERB CONJUGATION

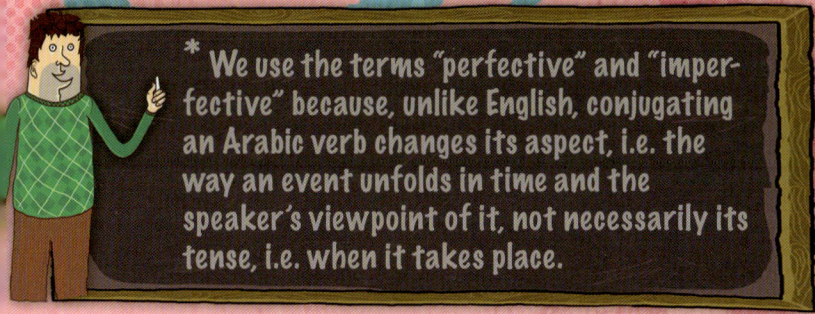

* We use the terms "perfective" and "imperfective" because, unlike English, conjugating an Arabic verb changes its aspect, i.e. the way an event unfolds in time and the speaker's viewpoint of it, not necessarily its tense, i.e. when it takes place.

We will begin by learning the imperfective stem, which itself has two major branches.

**Unmarked form:** Used like the infinitive (ex: "to be") in English, this form expresses possible or desirable actions.  It is also called the "subjunctive form".

**Marked form:** Indicates a general truth/assumed fact, or an intension.  This is also called the "indicative/intentive" form.

| Unmarked Imperfective | | Marked Imperfective | | |
|---|---|---|---|---|
| i + root | ا + فعل | b + root | بـ + فعل | أنا |
| t + ____ | تـ + ____ | bt + ____ | بتـ + ____ | إنتَ |
| t + ___ + i | تـ + ___ + ي | bt + ___ + i | بتـ + ___ + ي | إنتِ |
| y + ___ | يـ + ___ | by + ___ | بيـ + ___ | هوّ |
| t + ____ | تـ + ____ | bt + ____ | بتـ + ____ | هيّ |
| n + ____ | نـ + ____ | mn + ____ | منـ + ____ | نحنا |
| t + ___ + ou | تـ + ____ + و | bt + ___ + ou | بتـ + ____ + و | إنتو |
| y + ___ + ou | يـ + ____ + و | by + ___ + ou | بيـ + ____ + و | هنّ |

**Note:** Don't forget to put the prefix "m" instead of "b", when you conjugate the marked imperfective with "we".

Unmarked — يفعل
Imperfective Marked — بيفعل
Perfective-Past
Root — فعل

This is some new vocabulary we will be using to practice using verbs.
- We will always give you an example of new verbs' conjugation using the first person singular (أنا) marked imperfective form.

|  |  |  |
|---|---|---|
| To work (I work) | Shtaghal (Bishtighil) | شتغل ( بِشتغِل ) |
| To learn (I learn) | T3allam (Bit3allam) | تعلَّم ( بتعلَّم ) |
| To speak (I speak) | 7aka (Bi7ki) | حكى ( بِحكي ) |
| To know (I know) | 3irif (Ba3rif) | عرِف ( بَعرِف ) |
| To do/ make (I do) | 3imil (Ba3mol) | عمِل ( بعمُل ) |

|  |  |  |
|---|---|---|
| Every day | Kil yowm | كل يوم |
| A little bit | Shway | شوَي |

يلا نتمرن الأفعال الجديدة.
بسرعععععععععععععععة!!!!!

exercise

# Exercise 1.A :
## LANGUAGE PRACTICE

Match the verb with the situation.

| | |
|---|---|
| C | بيعرف |
| B | بيتعلم |
| A | منحكي |
| D | بيشتغلو |

A

D

B

C

# Exercise 2.A :
## LANGUAGE PRACTICE

Let's practice the marked conjugation of the new verbs. Fill in the missing conjugations below.

| | | | | | |
|---|---|---|---|---|---|
| أنا | بِشتغِل | بعرف | بتعلم | بحكي | يعمل |
| هوّ | بيشتغل | بيعرف | بيتعلم | بيحكي | بيعمِل |
| نحنا | منشتغل | منعرف | منتعلّم | منحكي | منعمل |
| إنتو | بتشتغلو بتعرفو | | بتتعلمو | بتحكو | بتعملو |
| هيّ | بتشتغل بتعرف | | بتتعلم | بتحكي | بتعمل |
| إنتَ | بتشتغل بتعرف | | بتتعلم | بتحكي | بتعمل |
| هنّ | بيشتغلو بيعرفو | | بيتعلمو | بيحكو | بيعملو |
| إنتِ | بتشتغلي | بتعرفي | بتتعلمي | بتحكي | بتعملي |

صفحة **48**

## B: HELPING VERBS

Helping verbs are conjugated like pseudo verbs using the pronoun suffix used to indicate the subject of the verb. Helping verbs always help explain another verb which comes directly after (e.g. "I want to learn", where helping verb = to want).

We will learn how to use badd (بدّ), and fi (في) as helping verbs, however, a regular verb can also be used to "help" another verb according to the following rule.

**Rule:**
Helping/marked verb + unmarked verb

SUBJECT    OBJECT    POSSESSION

| Want | Badd (baddi) | بدّ (بدّي) |
|------|--------------|-----------|
| Can  | Fi (fiye)    | في (فيّ) |

### Examples based on new grammar:

| | |
|---|---|
| Ni7na ma fina **n**ita3lim inglizi. | نحنا ما فينا **ن**تعلّم إنكليزي |
| Ana ma baddi **i**t3allam e7ki. | أنا ما بدي **إ**تعلّم إحكي |
| Huwwe baddoh **y**a3rif **y**e7ki 3arabi mnee7. | هو بده **ي**عرف **ي**حكي عربي منيح |

### Exercise 1.B :
## LANGUAGE PRACTICE

Choose one word from each column and add your own object from the nouns we have learned to create three different sentences.

| Subject | Helping verb | Unmarked verb |
|---------|--------------|---------------|
| نحنا | بد | عمل |
| جاد | في | حكى |
| إنتِ | | عرف |

نحنا بدنا نعمل إجتماع

جاد فيه يحكي لغات كتيرة

إنتِ طبدك تعرفي صدلن

## C: OCCUPATIONS
You don't need to memorize all of the occupations, just one or two that you need.

|  |  |
|---|---|
| Teacher (m - f - pl) | إِستاذ / مُعَلِمِة / أَسَاتِذِة |
| Doctor (m - f - pl) | دُكْتُور / دُكْتُورَة / دَكاتَرَة |
| Engineer (m - f - pl) | مُهَندِس / مُهَندْسِية / مُهَندْسِين |
| Student (m - f - pl) | طَالِب / طَالْبَة / طُلَّاب |
| Journalist (m - f - pl) | صَحَافِي / صَحَافِيّة / صَحَافِيين |
| Writer (m - f - pl) | كَاتِب / كَاتْبِة / كُتَّاب |
| Concierge (m - pl) | ناطُور / نَواطير |
| Manager (m - f - pl) | مُدير / مُديرَة / مُدَرا |
| Plumber (m - pl) | سَنكَري / سنكَرِية |
| President (m - f - pl) | رَئِيس / رَئِيسِة / رُؤَسَا |
| Employee (m - f - pl) | مُوَظَّف / مُوَظَّفِة / مُوَظَّفين |
| Artist (m - f - pl) | فَنَّان / فَنَّانِة / فَنَّانِين |
| Tailor ( m - f - pl) - w/ clothes | خَيَّاط / خَيَّاطَة / خَيَّاطين |
| Nurse (m - f - pl) | مُمَرِّض / مُمَرِّضَة / مُمَرِّضِين |
| House wife | سِت بَيْت |
| Photographer (m - f - pl) | مُصَوِّر / مُصَوَرَة / مُصَوُرين |
| Cook (m & f - pl) | شِيف / شِيفِيّة |
| Lawyer (m - f - pl) | مُحَامِي / مُحَامِيّة / مُحَامِيين |
| Carpenter (m - pl) | نَجَّار / نَجَّارين |
| Accountant (m - f - pl) | مُحَاسِب / مُحَاسْبِة / مُحَاسْبِين |
| Electrician (m - pl) | كَهْرَبَجي / كَهْرَبْجِية |

## Exercise 1.C :
## LANGUAGE PRACTICE

What are the workers doing?  Fill in the blanks with the correct verb and conjugation.

الشيف _____ أَكِل. (food)

هو _____ عالكمبيوتر.

الطّالب _____ بالمدرسة.

Bonjour!

الممرضة فيها _____ فرنسي.

Fill in the blanks with the correct conjugation of the given verb.

١-  سارة ـ_بتشتغل_ (شتغل) موظفة بشركة وكمان هي ـ_بتتعلم_ (تعلم) بال AUB.

٢-  جميل شيف ـ_بيعمل_ (عمل) أكل بمطعم جبران.

٣-  جاد و كارلا بدُّن ـ_يحكوا_ مع مديرُن (حكى).

٤-  جورج وكلارا ما فيُّن ـ_يشتغلوا_ (شتغل) هلأ عشان هن بالجامعة بس بدن ـ_يتعلموا يحكوا_ (تعلم) (حكى) عربي.

**Extra vocabulary:**
عشان = because - for - in order to

Read the following paragraph and underline all the verbs. Figure out who are the subjects of the verbs and write the verbs in the spaces below. If a verb refers to more than one subject write it under each subject.

أحمد كريم وناريمان بيشتغلو مهندسين بشركة "wehbi w alami". ناريمان كمان هي بتتعلّم بالجامعة بعد الضهُر بس كريم ما بيعمل شي بعد الضهر.

أحمد بيشتغل كمان مثل صحافي يعني part time. هو بيشتغل لـ Daily news.

| Ahmad | Karim | Nariman |
|---|---|---|
| بيشتغل | بيشتغل | بيشتغلو |
|  | ما بيعمل | بتتعلم |

# LANGUAGE DISCOVERY

These are some commonly used verbs... do you recognize them? If not try using them and find out what they mean. Conjugate them in the table below using badd ( بدّ )... Remember to use the unmarked form!

| | | |
|---|---|---|
| *to watch / attend* | 7idir (ana bi7dar) | حضَر ( أنا بحضَر) |
| *to strdy* | Darass (ana bidross) | درَس (أنا بدرُس) |
| *to come* | Ija (ana biji) | إجى (أنا بجي) |

| إجى | درس | حضر | |
|---|---|---|---|
| بدي إجي | بدي إدرس | بدي إحضَر فيلم | أنا |
| بدن يجو | بدن يدرسو | بدن يحضرو | هنّ |
| بدِك تجي | بدّك تدرسي عربي | بدِك تحضري | إنتِ |
| بده يجي | بده يدرس | بده يحضر | هوَ |
| بدكن تجو | بدكن تدرسو | بدكن تحضرو | إنتو |
| بدنا نجي عالصف | بدنا ندرس | بدنا نحضر | نحنا |
| بدها تجي | بدها تدرس | بدها تحضر | هي |
| بدَك تجي | بدَك تدرس | بدَك تحضر | إنتَ |

## Lesson review

After finishing this lesson and practicing inside and outside the class you should be able to:
- Conjugate verbs in the imperfective tense
- Use verbs with helping verbs
- Ask people about their occupations and identify your own

**A: NUMBERS 0-12**

| ٠ صفر |
|---|

| ٤ أربَعَة | ٣ تلاِتة | ٢ تنَين | ١ واحَد |
|---|---|---|---|
| ٨ تمانِة | ٧ سبعَة | ٦ ستِّة | ٥ خمسِة |
| ١٢ تنَعش | ١١ حدِعش | ١٠ عشرَة | ٩ تسعَة |

## Vocabulary        المفردات

| Number / (pl) | Ra2m / ar2am | رقم / أرقام |
| Phone number | Ra2m telephone | رقم تلفون |
| Licence plate | Ra2m siyarah | رقم السيارة |

## Exercise 1.A :
# LANGUAGE DISCOVERY

Play for fun & finish this Sudoku with Arabic numbers.

| ٤ | ١ | ٢ | ٦ | ٥ | ٣ | ٧ | ٩ | ٨ |
|---|---|---|---|---|---|---|---|---|
| ٥ | ٣ | ٦ | ٧ | ٩ | ٨ | ٢ | ٤ | ١ |
| ٩ | ٨ | ٧ | ٢ | ٤ | ١ | ٦ | ٥ | ٣ |
| ٨ | ٦ | ٤ | ٥ | ١ | ٧ | ٩ | ٣ | ٢ |
| ١ | ٧ | ٩ | ٤ | ٣ | ٢ | ٧ | ٨ | ٦ |
| ٣ | ٢ | ٥ | ٩ | ٨ | ٦ | ٤ | ١ | ٧ |
| ٧ | ٤ | ٣ | ٨ | ٧ | ٥ | ١ | ٢ | ٩ |
| ٧ | ٥ | ٨ | ١ | ٢ | ٩ | ٣ | ٦ | ٤ |
| ٢ | ٩ | ١ | ٣ | ٦ | ٤ | ٨ | ٧ | ٥ |

First, write out each number of your phone number, then ask your friends or class-mates what their phone number is ("shou ra2amak?") and write out each number.

رقمي صفر تلاتة ...

رقم صفر تلاتة أربعة تسعة ستة تمانة واحد

رقم

رقم

Write out each number of the following Lebanese licence places:

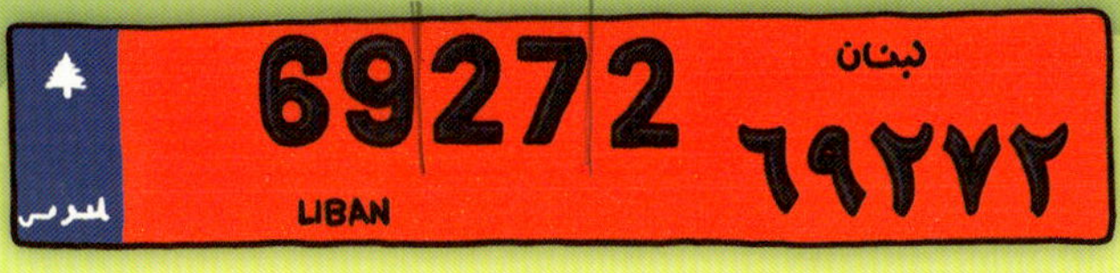

| لبنان 69272 ٦٩٢٧٢ LIBAN | لبنان 572 ٥٧٢ LIBAN |
|---|---|

تسعة ميتين الف و | ثمان مية / أحمية

ميتين وتنين وسبعين | وتنين وسبعين

| What time is it? | Addeish sa3ah? | أديش الساعة؟ |
| When? | Aymta? | أيمتى؟ |
| When_____ | Lamma_____ | لمّا_____ |
| At what time (Which time?) | Ayya sa3ah? | أيّ ساعة؟ |
| Time | Wa2it | وقت |
| Hour (watch, clock) / (pl) | Sa3ah / sa3at | ساعة / ساعات |
| Minute / (pl) | D2ee2ah / da2ayi2 | دقيقة / دقايق |
| Exactly | Bizzabit | بالظبط |
| Almost (about) | Ta2riban | تقريباً |
| Half | Noss | نص |
| Third | Tilit | تلت |
| Quarter | Robo3 | ربع |
| And | Wa (wo) | و |
| Minus (i.e. "It is 3 o'clock minus 10 minutes") | ella | إلّا |
| From _____ until_____ | Min_____ la_____ | مِن_____ لـ_____ |
| See you (m/f) | Bshoufak / Bshoufik | بشوفَك / بشوفِك |

الساعة تسعة و نص

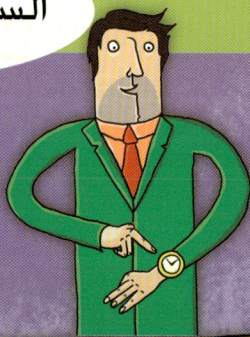

أديش السَّاعة؟

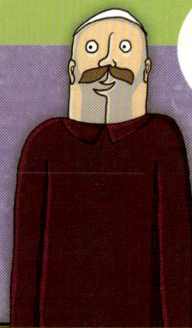

**Note:** The time of day is said like this: Three o'clock = الساعة تلاتة
There are two exceptions:

One o'clock = الساعة و حدة, two o'clock = الساعة تنتين

How full are these cups?

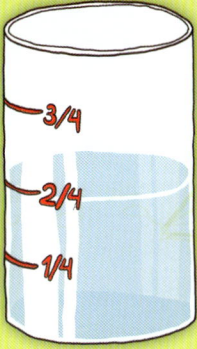

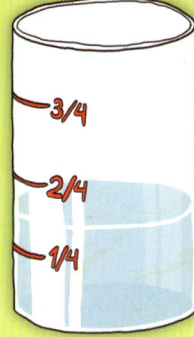

نص

زيج

كلك

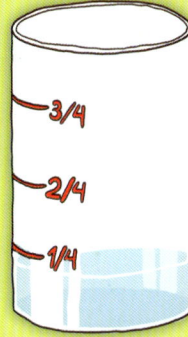

تقريبا نص

تقريبا ربج

Read the following questions and answer in Arabic using your new verbs.

من أيّ ساعة لأي ساعة بتشتغل؟ ـ بشتغل من الساعة ثمانية للساعة خمسة

أي ساعة بتحضر تلفزيون؟ ـ بحضر تلفزيون عالساعة عشرة

أي ساعة بتجي عصف العربي؟ ـ بجي صف العربي عالساعة تسعة

أيمتى بتدرس؟ ـ بحب إدرس عالساعة عشرة صباحاً

مساء/الليل (night)

Read the following times and draw the clock that matches the time.

الساعة ٩ : ٣٥

الساعة ١٠ : ٤٥

الساعة ٧ : ٢٠

الساعة ١٢:١٥

الساعة تلاتة ونص إلّا خمسة

Try to find in Arabic the meaning of "am, pm" and write them below.

| | |
|---|---|
| _____ | _____ |

## C: PAST TENSE OF HELPING AND PSEUDO VERBS

It's very easy to use helping/pseudo verbs in the past tense.
You just need to add one word and voila, it's past tense!

### Kan (كان) + helping/pseudo verb = past tense

**Example:** i had a house = كان عندي بيت

### Exercise 1.C :
## LANGUAGE PRACTICE

Let's finish conjugation of verb "badd and 3ind" in past tense.

| كان عندي | كان بدي | أنا |
|---|---|---|
| كان عندَك | كان بدك | إنتَ |
| كان عندِك | كان بدِك | إنتِ |
| كان عنده | كان بده | هوّ |
| كان عندها | كان بدها | هي |
| كان عندنا | كان بديا | نحنا |
| كان عندكن | كان بدكن | إنتو |
| كان عندن | كان بدن | هن |

## Exercise 2.C :
## *LANGUAGE PRACTICE*

**Write the questions of the following answers in Arabic.**

| | | |
|---|---|---|
| هو كان بدّه يعرف مين هيدي. | ؟ | شو كان بدّه يعرف |
| هي ما كان بدا شي. | ؟ | شو كان بدا |
| ما كان عندنا صف. بس عندنا شغُل. | ؟ | كان عندكن صف |
| هن ما كان عندُن شغُل. | ؟ | كان عندن شغل |

## Exercise 3.C :
## *LANGUAGE PRACTICE*

**Translate the following sentences in Arabic.**

| | |
|---|---|
| I don't want to watch tv. | ما بدي إحضر التلفزيون |
| You (m) don't want to watch tv. | انك ما بدك تحضر التلفزيون |
| He didn't want to watch tv. | ما كان بده يحضر |
| She didn't want to come home. | ما كان بدها تجي البيت |
| We didn't want to come to class every day. | ما كان بدنا نجي عالصف كل يوم |
| They didn't want to speak at work. | ما كان بدن يحكو بالشغل |
| Do you (pl) want to learn how to speak in Arabic? | بدكن تتعلمو كيف تحكو عربي |

| | |
|---|---|
| I want to learn how to speak in Arabic. | بدي إتعلم كيف إحكي بالعربي |
| She wants to learn how to speak in Arabic. | بدها تتعلم كيف تحكي بالعربي |
| He didn't want to learn English. | ما كان بده يتعلم إنجليزي |
| We didn't want to work here. | ما كان بدنا نشتغل هون |
| She doesn't want to come to work by car. | ما كان بدها تجي عالشغل بالسيارة |
| Why you (f) didn't want to watch this movie? | ليش ما كان بدك تتفرجي هيدا الفيلم |
| Why didn't they want to know his name? | ليش ما كان بدن يعرفو إسمه؟ |
| He doesn't have class every day. | ما عنده صف كل يوم |

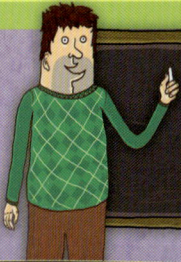

**Extra Vocabulary:**
Why? = leish? ليش؟

## Exercise 4.C :
# LANGUAGE PRACTICE

Change the following passage from the personal pronoun "he" to "she". Be sure to make all necessary changes. Then write similar paragraph talking about yourself, using all the words and verbs that you have learned until now.

هو إسمُه رامي جابر. هو بيشتغل كل يوم بالجريدة العربية. هو بيحكي عربي وفرنسي بس ما بيعرف يحكي إنكليزي عشان هو بيدرس كمان بجامعة USJ وهونيك الطلاب بيتعلمو يحكو فرنسي و عربي بس. هو عنده بيت وسيارة وتلفون وكومبيوتر. بيتُه بالحمرا حد مطعم مروش. لمّا بيجي من شغلُه. بيحضر تلفزيون وبيدرس شوي.
هو كان بدّه يشتغل مدير لمدرسة بس هلّأ عنده شغُل كتير منيح.

هي إسمها هنادي جابر. هي بتشتغل كل يوم بالجريدة العربية. هي بتحكي عربي وفرنسي بس ما بتعرف تحكي إنكليزي عشان هي بتدرس كمان بجا USJ وهونيك الطلاب بيتعلمو يحكو فرنسي و عربي بس. هي عندها بيت وسيارة و بيتها بالحمرا حد مطعم مروش. لما بتجي من شغلها. بتحضر تلفزيون وبتدرس شوي. هي كان بدها تشتغل مدير لمدرسة بس هلا عندها شغل كبير

About yourself:

### Lesson review

After finishing this lesson and practicing inside and outside class you should be able to:
- Count to 12
- Talk about the time
- Make simple past tense sentences using helping verbs and pseudo verbs

مع السلامة
See you in book 2

# WORD REFERENCE

|  |  |  |
|---------|----------------|--------|
| Able to / Can | fee+__ | في+____ |
| Above (over, up) | Fow2 | فوق |
| Accountant (m- f- pl) | mo7assib /eh / een | مُحاسِب / مُحَاسبة / مُحَاسبين |
| After | Ba3id | بعد |
| All, every, each | Kill | كِلُ |
| Almost (about) | Ta2riban | تقريباً |
| Always | Dayman | دايماً |
| And… | Wo or wa | و |
| Arabic Pizza | Man2ousheh/ mana2eesh | مَنقوشة/ مَنَاقيش |
| Article | ma2al/ ma2alat | مقال/ مقالات |
| Artist (m- f- pl) | fannan / fannaneh / fannaneen | فتان / فنانة / فنانين |
| At (someone's place) | 3ind | عند |
| Bag | shantah/ shonat | شنتة/ شُنَت |
| Because / for / in order to | 3ashan | عشان |
| Before | Abel | قبل |
| Behind | Wara | ورا |
| Between | Bayn | بين |
| Bill (account) | 7ssab | حساب |
| Book | ktab/ kotob | كتَاب/ كُتُب |
| Box / cash register | Sandou2/ sanadi2 | صندوق/ صناديق |
| Building | binayeh/ binayat | بناية/ بنايات |
| Busy (m- f- pl) | Mashghoul / eh/ een | مشْغول / ة / ين |
| But, only, enough, just | Bass | بس |
| Buy | Shtara (ana bishtiri) | (شترى أنا بِشتري) |
| Bye: Do you(m) need anything before I leave? | Baddak shi? | بدَّك شي؟ |
| Bye: Excuse me (Making sure that it's ok to leave) | Bil 2izin | بالإذن. |
| Bye: God bless you (m) | Allah yssalmak | الله يسلمَك. |
| Bye: Have a safe trip (when someone else leaves) | Ma3 salameh | مع السلامة. |
| Bye: May god reward you too | Allah y3afik. | الله يعافيك. |
| Bye: May god reward you with good health | Ya3tik l3afyeh | يعطيك العافية |
| Cake (round Arabic bread with a hole in the middle) | Ka3keh/ ka3kat | كعكِة/ كعكات |
| Call (to phone) | Tassal b+ (noun) /fee+ (pr) | تصَل بـ+ (إسم)/ في+ (ضمير) |
| Car | siyarah/ siyarat | سيارَة/ سيارات |
| Carpenter (m- f- pl) | Najjar /ah / een | نجّار/ نجارة/ نجّارين |
| Cash register / box | Sandou2/ sanadi2 | صندوق/ صناديق |
| Celebrate | 7tafal (ana bi7tifil) | حتفَل (أنا بِحتفِل) |
| Chair | kirsseh/ karassi | كرسي/ كراسي |
| Chef (m- f- pl) | Tabbakh/ ah/ een | طبّاخ / طباخة / طبّاخين |
| Chestnut | Kasstana | كستنا |
| Class | saf/ sfouf | صفُ |
| Clock / watch / hour | sa3ah/ sa3at | ساعة / ساعات |
| Come | Ija (ana biji) | إجى (أنا بجي) |
| Company / (pl) | Shirkeh / sharikat | شركة / شركات |
| Computer | computer/ computerat | كومبيوتر/ كومبيوترات |
| Concierge (m- f- pl) | Natour / Natourah / Nawateer | ناطور / ناطورة / نواطير |
| Cook (I cook) | Tabakh (botbokh) | طبخ (بَطبُخ) |
| Corn | 3arnous/ 3aranees | عرنوس/ عرانيس |
| Couch | kanabayeh/ kanabayat | كنباية/ كنبايات |
| Cup / glass | kibayeh/ kibayat | كبّاية / كبّايات |
| Depends | 7assab (ma) | حسَب (ما) |

|  |  |  |
|---|---|---|
| Descend (go down), to stay (in a place) | Nizil (ana binzal) | نِزِل (أنا بنزَل) |
| Do (I do) | 3imil (ba3mol) | عمل (بعمَل) |
| Doctor (m- f- pl) | Doctor / doctorah / dakatrah | دكتور / دكتورة /دكاترة |
| Drink | Shirib (ana bishrab) | شِرِب (أنا بِشرَب) |
| Early | Bakkir | بكّير |
| Eat | Akal (ana bakol) | أكل (أنا باكُل) |
| Eight | Tmaneh | 8 / تمانة |
| Eleven | 7da3ish | 11 / حدعش |
| Employee (m- f- pl) | Mwazzaf/ eh/ een | موظّف / موظفة / موظفين |
| Empty (free) (m- f- pl) | Fadi / eh/ een | فاضي / ة/ ين |
| Engineer (m- f- pl) | Mhandiss/seh/ een | مهندس / مهندِسية / مهندسيين |
| Enough, but, only, just | Bass | بس |
| Every day | Kil yowm | كل يوم |
| Everything is fine | Mashi l7al | ماشي الحَال |
| Everything is perfect | Kill shi tamam | كل شي تمام |
| Exactly | Bizzabit | بالظبط |
| Except for | Ma 3ada | ما عَدا |
| Far from | B3eed 3an | بعيد عن |
| Fast | Bissir3ah | بسرعَة |
| Finish | Khallass (bkhalliss) | خلّص (بخلّص) |
| Five | Khamsseh | خمسة / 5 |
| Food | Akil | أكل |
| For / because / in order to | 3ashan | عشان |
| Four | Arb3ah | أربعَة / 4 |
| From _____ until | Min_____ la | مِن ـــــــــــــ لـ |
| Go | Ra7 (brou7) | راح ( بروح) |
| Go ahead (m/f/pl) | Tfadall/ tfadali/ tfadalou | تفضّل/ تفضّلي/ تفضّلو |
| Go out | Dahar (bidhar) | ضَهَر (يضهر) |
| Good, fine (m-f-pl) | Mnee7/ mnee7a/ mnai7 | منيح / منيحة/مناح |
| Half | Noss | نص |
| He | Huwwi | هوّ |
| Heater | daffayeh/ daffayat | دفّاية/ دفّايات |
| Hello (double) | Mar7abtein | مرحبتين |
| Here / there | Hon/ honik | هون / هونيك |
| Hers | Taba3ah / Elah | إلا / تبعا |
| Hi (hello) | Mar7aba | مرحَبا |
| Hi (Welcome) | Ahlein | أهلين |
| Hi (Welcome) | Ahlan wa sahlan | أهلاً و سهلاً |
| His | Taba3oh / Eloh | إلَه / تبعُه |
| Hospital | Mostashfa/ mostashfayat | مستشفى / مستشفيات |
| Hour (watch, clock) / (pl) | Sa3ah / sa3at | ساعة / ساعات |
| House | bayt / byout | بَيت / بيوت |
| House wife | Sit bayt | ست بيت |
| How are you (m-f-pl)? | Keefak/ keefik/ keefkon? | كيفَك/ كيفِك/ كيفكُن؟ |
| How? | Keef? | كيف؟ |
| How's it going? | Keef l7al? | كيف الحَال؟ |
| How's your health (m)? | Keef sa7tak? | كيف صحتَك ؟ |
| Hurry up / lets go | Yalla | يلّا |
| I | Ana | أنا |
| In (place), & with (things) | Bi | بـ |

# WORD REFERENCE

|  |  |  |
|---|---|---|
| In + pronouns suffix | Fee+_____ | في+_____ |
| In front (across) | Eddam(biwij) | إدّام |
| Journalist (m- f- pl) | Sa7afee/ yeh/ yeen | صَحَافي / صحَافية / صحافيين |
| Juice | 3asseer | عصير |
| Just, but, only, enough | Bass | بس |
| Kitchen | Matbakh / matabikh | مطبخ / مَطابِخ |
| Know | 3irif (ana ba3rif) | عرف (أنا بَعرف) |
| Late (m- f- pl) | Mit2akhir / ah/ een | متأخِّر / ة / ين |
| Lawyer (m- f- pl) | Mo7ami/ eh/ een | محامي / محامية / محاميين |
| Learn (I learn) | T3allam (bit3allam) | تعلَّم (بتعلَّم) |
| Let's go / hurry up | Yalla | يلا |
| Listen | Simi3 (ana bisma3) | سمع (أنا بِسمَع) |
| Little bit | Shway | شوَي |
| Live (in a place) | Sakan (ana biskon) | سكَن (أنا بسكُن) |
| Look at | Tfarraj 3a( ana bitfarraj 3a) | تفرّج على (أنا بتفرّج على) |
| Manager (m- f- pl) | modeer/ah/ modara | مُدير / مُديرة / مُدرا |
| Master / Professor | istaz/ m3allmeh/ assatzeh | إستاذ / معلمة / أساتذة |
| Maybe, perhaps | Yimkin | يمكِن |
| Mine | Taba3i / Eli | إلي / تبعي |
| Minus (i.e. "It is 3 o'clock minus 10 minutes") | 2ella | إلّا |
| Minute / (pl) | D2i2ah / da2ayi2 | دقيقة / دقايق |
| Morning | Sobo7 | الصُّبح |
| Mug | finjan/ fanajeen | فنجان/ فناجين |
| My name is… | Issmi…. | إسمي…. |
| Near by | Areeb min | قريب من |
| Neither _____ nor _____ | La _____ wala_____ | لا_____ ولا_____ |
| Never | Abadan | أبداً |
| Newspaper | jareedeh/ jarayid | جريدة / جرَايِد |
| Next to (beside) | 7ad | حد |
| Nice to meet you | Tcharrafna | تشرّفنا |
| Night | Layl | الليل |
| Nine | Tiss3ah | 9 / تسعَة |
| No | La | لا |
| No longer, not anymore | Ma ba2a | ما بقى |
| Nobody | Ma 7ada | ما حدا / ولا واحد |
| Noon | Dohor | الضّهُر |
| No-one | wala wa7ad | ولا واحَد |
| Not + (nouns & adj) | Mish | مش |
| Notebook | daftar/ dafatir | دفتر/ دفاتِر |
| Nothing new | Ma shi jdeed | ما شي جديد |
| Nurse (m- f- pl) | Momarid/ ah/ een | ممرّض / مُمرّضة / ممرضين |
| Of course, for sure, definitely | Akeed. | أكيد |
| One | Wa7ad | واحَد / 1 |
| Only, but, enough, just | Bass | بس |
| Ours | Taba3na / Elna | إلنا / تبعنا |
| Peace upon you | Assalamu 3alaykom | السَّلام عليكم |
| Pen | alam/ 2lam | قَلَم/ قلام |
| Picture | sourah/ sowar | صورة/ صُوَر |
| Play | Li3ib (bil3ab) | لِعب (بِلعب) |
| Peace be upon you (response) | Wa 3alaykom assalam | وعليكم السلام. |

# WORD REFERENCE

|  |  |  |
|---|---|---|
| Please: Do me a favor (m/ f/ pl) | 3mol/ 3meli / 3melou ma3rouf… | عمول/ عملي/ عملو معروف... |
| Please: If you (m/ f/ pl) permit | Law sama7t/ sama7ti/ sama7tou… | لو سمحت/ سمحتي/ سمحتو... |
| Please: If you accept (m/f/ pl) | Iza bitreed/ bitreedi/ bitreedou… | إذا بتريد/ بتريدي/ بتريدو... |
| Please: Of your generosity (m/f/pl) | Min fadlak/ fadlik/ fadlkon… | من فضلَك/ فضلك/ فضلكُن... |
| Plumber (m- f- pl) | Sankri/ eh/ een | سنكري / سنكرية / سنكربين |
| Police (m- f- pl) | Shorti/ eh/ een | شُرطي / شُرطية / شرطة |
| Praise god | L7mdillah | الحمدلله |
| President (m- f- pl) | Ra2eess/ eh/ ro2assa | رئيس / رئيسة / رُؤسا |
| Professor / master | istaz/ m3almeh/ assatzeh | إستاذ / معلمة / أساتذة |
| Quarter | Robo3 | ربع |
| Read (I read) | 2ara (bi2ra) | قرا (بقرا) |
| Report | Ta2reer/ ta2areer | تقرير/ تقارير |
| Seven | Sab3ah | سبعَة / 8 |
| She | Hiyyi | هي |
| Six | Sitteh | ستِّة / 6 |
| Sleep | Nam (bnam) | نام (بنام) |
| Sometime | A7yanan | أحياناً |
| So-so, I mean… | Ya3ni | يعني |
| Start (I start) | Ballash (biballish) | بلَّش (بُبَلِّش) |
| Stay (in a place), to go down (descend) | Nizil (ana binzal) | نزل (أنا بنزَل) |
| Stay up late | Sihir (bishar) | سهِر (بسهَر) |
| Street | shari3/ shawari3 | شارع/ شوارع |
| Student (m- f- pl) | Talib/ talbeh/ tollab | طالب / طالبة / طلاب |
| Study | Darass (ana bidross) | درَس (أنا بدرُس) |
| Table | Tawleh/ tawlat | طاولة/ طاولات |
| Tailor ( m- f- pl) | khayyat/ khayyatah/ khayyateen | خياط / خياطة / خياطين |
| Take | Akhad (ana bakhod) | أخد (أنا باخُد) |
| Teacher (m- f- pl) | m3almeh/ isstaz/ assatzeh | إستاذ / معلمة / أساتذة |
| Telephone | telephone/ telephonat | تلفون/ تلفونات |
| Ten | 3ashrah | 10 / عشرَة |
| Thanks | Shukran/ yisslamou | شكراً / يسلمو |
| Theirs | Taba3on / Elon | إلن / تبعن |
| These (pl) | haydol | هيدول |
| They | Hinni | هن |
| Third | Tilit | تلت |
| This (f) | haydi | هيدي |
| This (m) | Hayda | هيدا |
| Three | Tlateh | تلاتة / 3 |
| Time | Wa2it/ aw2at | وقت |
| Tired (m- f- pl) | Ta3ban / eh/ een | تعبان / ة / ين |
| To (on) | 3a (3ala) | ء (على) |
| To (someone) | La____ | لـ____ |
| To, or for (someone) | La____ | لـ____ |
| Travel | Safar (bssafir) | سافر (بسافر) |
| Twelve | Tna3ish | تنَعش / 12 |
| Two | Tnayn | تنَين / 2 |
| Under (below, down) | Ta7t | تحت |
| Usually | 3adatan | عادةً |
| Very good (m) … | Kteer mnee7…. | كتير منيح.. |
| Wake up | Fa2 (bfee2) | فاق (بفيق) |

# WORD REFERENCE

|  |  |  |
|---|---|---|
| Walet | jizdan/ jazadeen | جزدان / جزادين |
| Want (verb) | Badd+__ | ____+بدّ |
| Was | Kan | كان |
| Watch, attend | 7idir (ana bi7dar) | حضر ( أنا بحضَر) |
| Water | Mai | ماي |
| We | Ni7na | نحنا |
| Welcome (Hi) | Ahlein | أهلين |
| Welcome (Hi) | Ahlan wa sahlan | أهلاً و سهلاً |
| Welcome (response to please): You (m/f/pl) are welcome | Tikram/ tikrami/ tikramou | تكرّم/ تكرّمي/ تكرّمو |
| Welcome (response to please): You(m/f/pl) are full of manners | Killak/ killik/ kilkon zow2 | كلّك/ كلّك/ كلكُن ذوق |
| What time is it? | Addeish sa3ah? | أديش الساعة؟ |
| What? | Shou? | شو؟ |
| What's your name (m-f)? | Shou issmak/ issmik? | شو إسمَك/ إسمِك؟ |
| What's your news (f)? | Shou akhbarik? | شو أخبارك ؟ |
| When (i.e. when I win) | Lamma | لمّا |
| When? | Aymta? | أيمتى؟ |
| Where? | Wein? | وين؟ |
| Which time? | Ayya sa3ah? | أيَّ ساعة؟ |
| Who does _____ belong to? | Lameen _____? | لمين _____؟ |
| Who's? | Meen? | مين؟ |
| With (people) | Ma3 | مع |
| Without | Bidoun/ bala | بدون/ بلا |
| Work | shoghl | شغُل |
| Work (I work) | Shataghal (bishtighil) | شتغل (بشتغِل) |
| Write (I write) | Katab (biktob) | كتب (بكتُب) |
| Writer (m- f- pl) | Katib/ katbeh/ kottab | كاتب / كاتبة / كُتاب |
| Yes | Eh | إي |
| You (f) | Inti | إنتِ |
| You (m-f-pl) | Inta - Inti - Intou | إنتَ- إنتِ- إنتو |
| You(m) | Inta | إنتَ |
| You(pl) | Intou | إنتو |
| Yours(f) | Elik / Taba3ik | إلِك / تبعِك |
| Yours(m) | Elak / Taba3ak | إلَك / تبعَك |
| Yours(pl) | Elkon / Taba3kon | إلكن / تبعكن |
| Zero | Sifir | صفر / 0 |

## Answers

| Page | Exercise | Answer (Latin) | Answer (Arabic) | Alt. Answer |
|---|---|---|---|---|
| 9 | 1.A | A- Mar7aba — B- Ahlein | ب- أهلين / أ- مرحبا | B- Ahlein |
| | | A-Mar7aba — B- Ahlan wa sahlan | ب- أهلاً وسهلاً / أ- مرحبا | B- Ahlan wa sahlan |
| | | A- Assalamu 3alaykom — B- Wa 3alaykom assalam | ب- وعليكم السلام / أ- السلام عليكم | B- Wa 3alaykom assalam |
| 10 | 2.A | A- Ya3tik l3afyeh — B- Allah y3afik | ب- الله يعافيك / أ- يعطيك العافية | B- Allah y3afik |
| | 3.A | Hamra | Achrafieh | Da7yeh |
| | | | | Jabal |
| 12 | 1.B | A- Mar7aba/ B- ahlein | ب- أهلين | B- Ahlein |
| | | A- Keefak/ B- mnee7 | ب- الحمدلله | A- Mar7aba/ B- Mar7abtein |
| | | A- Mar7aba isstaz | ب- أهلين حبيبتي | A- Keefik/ B- Mnee7 l7amdella |
| | | A- Keefak, shou akhbarak? | ب- L7amdillah | B- L7amdillah |
| | | A- Mar7aba ya 7elweh. | ب- الحمدلله. تمام | B- Ahlein 7abibti. |
| | | A- Keefik, mnee7a? | ب- مرحبتين | B- L7amdillah, tamam. |
| | | A- Mar7aba ya 7elo! | | B- Mar7abtein |
| | | A- Keefak, mnee7? | ب- ماشي الحال. الحمدلله | B- Mashi l7al, l7amdillah. |
| 13 | 1.C | A- Mar7aba | ب- أهلين | B- Ahlein |
| | | A- KeefiK? | ب- منيحة الحمدلله وإنت؟ | B- Mnee7a, l7amdillah w inta? |
| | | A- L7amdillah tamam.Shou issmik? | ب- إسمي ريما وإنت؟ | B- Issmi Rima, w inta? |
| | | A- Tcharrafna Rima, ana Tom. | ب- تشرفنا توم. | B- Tcharrafna Tom. |
| 16 | 1.D | Rita- Mar7aba Diala | Diala- Ahlein rita keefik? | |
| | | Rita- Mnee7a lhamdillah, w inti? | Diala- Mashi l7al, tamam.shou akhbarik? | |
| | | Rita- Ma shi jdeed.keef sa7tik? | Diala- Tamam l7amdillah | |
| | | Rita- Yalla baddik shi? | Diala- La, ma3 salameh | |
| | | Marwan- Mar7aba, ya3tik l3afyeh isstaz Hamid. | Isstaz Hamid- Ahlein, alla y3afik marwan. Keefak, mnee77?! | |
| | | Marwan-Kteer mnee7, l7amdillah w inta? | Isstaz Hamid-L7amdillah, tamam. Yalla bil 2izn Marwan. | |
| | | Marwan- Iznak ma3ak isstaz, Ma3 salameh. | Isstaz Hamid- Allah yssalmak, bye. | |
| | | Hayda Tony? | La, hayda mish Tony , hayda Moustapha. | |
| | | Haydi Diala? | la, haydi mish Diala , haydi Aline. | |
| | | Meen hayda? | Hayda Hamid. | |
| 18 | 1.A | Hayda mish Bob? | La, hayda mish Bob. | |
| | | Haydi Diala? | La, haydi mish Diala, haydi Noura. | |
| | | Meen haydi? | Haydi Aline. | |
| | | Haydi Noura? | La, haydi mish Noura, haydi Rita. | |
| | | Hayda Bob? | Eh, hayda Bob. | |
| 19 | 2.A | Nouhad Haddad was born on the 21st of November 1935, and is famously known as Feiruz. She is an old Lebanese singer, considered as a cultural icon of the Arab world. All the lebanese and Arab world listen to Feiruz in the morning, because of her songs, that give a good and fresh feeling. | | |
| 20 | 3.A | Shou hayda? | Hayda bayt. — هيدا بيت. | |
| | | Shou hayda? | Hayda alam. — هيدا قلم. | |
| | | Shou hayda? | Hayda ktab. — هيدا كتاب. | |

| Page | Exercise | | | | |
|---|---|---|---|---|---|
| | | Shou hayda? | شو هيدا؟ | Hayda maktab. | هيدا مكتب. |
| 22 | 4.A | Shou hayda? | شو هيدا؟ | Hayda daftar. | هيدا دفتر. |
| | | Shou haydi? | شو هيدي؟ | haydi arghuileh. | هيدي ارغيلة. |
| | | Masculine | مذكّر | Feminine | مؤنّث |
| | | Bed = Takhit | تخت | Traffic = 3aj2ah | عجقة |
| | | Schedule = Birnamij | برنامج | Party = 7afleh | حفلة |
| | | Meeting = Ijtima3 | اِجتماع | Interview = Mo2abaleh | مقابلة |
| | | Restaurant = Mat3am | مَطعم | Coffee = Ahweh | قهوة |
| 24 | 1.B | 1) Huwwe | هوّ (1 | | |
| | | 2) Hiyye | هيّ (2 | | |
| | | 3) Hinne | هنّ (3 | | |
| | | 4) ___Oh | ك (4 | | |
| | | 5) ___Ha / a | ها / ـها (6 | | |
| | | 6) ___Hon / on | ـهن / ـن (7 | | |
| | 2.B | ktaboh | كتابه | Huwwe | هوّ |
| | | Alamon | قلمن | Hinne | هنّ |
| | | Shoghlah | شغلة | Hiyye | هيّ |
| | | Maktabkon | مكتبكن | Intou | اِنتو |
| | | M3almitna | معلّمتنا | Ni7na | نحنا |
| | | Issmak | اِسمك | Inta | اِنت |
| | | Siyarti | سيّارتي | Ana | انا |
| | | Isstazik | اِستاذك | Inti | اِنتِ |
| 26 | 1.C | Hayda finjani. | هيدا فنجاني. | | |
| | | Hayda mish daftaroh. | هيدا مش دفتره. | | |
| | | Haydi shantitah. | هيدي شنتيتها. | | |
| | | Haydi m3almitna. | هيدي معلّمتنا. | | |
| | | Hayda baytak? | هيدا بيتك؟ | | |
| | | Hayda isstazon. | هيدا اِستاذن. | | |
| | | Haydi kirsstik? | هيدي كرسّتك؟ | | |
| | | Haydi jareeditkon? | هيدي جريدتكن؟ | | |
| | | Haydi tawltoh. | هيدي طاولتُه. | | |
| | | Haydi siyarti. | هيدي سيّارتي. | | |
| | | Haydi sa3itah. | هيدي ساعتها. | | |
| | | Hayda finjanoh? | هيدا فنجانه. | | |
| | | Haydi shanttak. | هيدي شنتّك. | | |
| | | Haydi shanttik. | هيدي شنتّك. | | |
| 27 | 2.C | His: Kibbaytoh, finjanoh, saffoh. | أهدّ: كتابُه، فنجانُه، صفُّه. | | |

# ANSWERS

| Page | Exercise | | |
|---|---|---|---|
| | | Their: bayton, shoghlon, m3almiton. | أبن: بيتُن شُغلُن معلمِتُن |
| | | Your (pl): sa3itkon, shogholkon, alamkon. | إلكن: ساعتكن شُغلكن علمكُن |
| | | Our: isstazna, baytna, shantitna. | إلنا: إستاذنا بيتنا شنتيتنا |
| | | Her: issma, kirssita, siyarita. | إلها: إسمه كرسيته سياره |
| | | My: shantti, m3almti, kibbayti. | إلي: شنتي معلمتي كبايتي |
| 29 | 3.C | Haydi siyarita. | هيدي سيارتا. |
| | | Hayda maktaboh. | هيدا مكتبه. |
| | | Hayda eli. | هيدا إلي. |
| | | Hayda bayta. | هيدا بيتا. |
| | | Haydi elna. | هيدي إلنا. |
| | | Hayda elon. | هيدا إلون. |
| | | Haydi eli. | هيدي إلي. |
| 30 | 4.C | Hayda ktabak? | هيدا كتابك؟ |
| | | Hayda baytkon? | هيدا بيتكن؟ |
| | | Lameen haydi siyarah? | لمين هيدي سيارة؟ |
| | | Haydi ljareedeh elon? | هيدي الجريدة إلون؟ |
| | | Lameen haydi lkibbayeh? | لمين هيدي الكبايه؟ |
| | | Haydi m3almitkon? | هيدي معلمتكن؟ |
| | | Hayda isstazkon? | هيدا إستاذكن؟ |
| | | Hayda daftar mish eloh?! | هيدا الدفتر مش إله؟! |
| | | Haydi siyariton? | هيدي سيارتُن؟ |
| | | Haydi ardoh? | هيدي أرضه؟ |
| | | Haydi siyarit lim3almeh? | هيدي سيارة المعلمة؟ |
| | | Lameen haydol l2alam w daftar? | لمين هيدول القلم والدفتر؟ |
| | | Hayda ktaboh? | هيدا كتابه؟ |
| | | Lameen haydol lktab w shantah? | لمين هيدول الكتاب والشنتة؟ |
| 31 | 5.C | Saffoh | صفّه |
| | | Isstaza | إستاذا |
| | | Finjana | فنجانا |
| | | Elik | إلك |
| | | Hayda | هيدا |
| 32 | 1.A | using genitive construction to indicate possession | |
| | | 1: Hayda sa7ib Shirine. | 1: هيدا صاحب شيرين. |
| | | 2: Haydol rif2at kamal. | 2: هيدول رفقات كمال. |
| | | using pronoun suffix to indicate possession | |
| | | 1: Haydi sa7ibtoh. | 1: هيدي صاحبته. |
| | | 2: Haydol massariha. | 2: هيدول مصاريها. |

**Page  Exercise**

| Page | Exercise | |
|---|---|---|
| 34 | 1.B | Section 1, from left to right. — القِسم الأوّل، من اليمين للشمال. |
| | | Man2ousheh - mana2eesh — مَنْقوشة - مَناقيش |
| | | 3arnouss - 3araneess — عَرنوس - عَرانيس |
| | | Ka3keh - ka3ik — كَعْكة - كَعِك |
| | | Kasstana — كَسْتَنة |
| | | 3assir laymoun — عَصير لَيْمون |
| | | Anneenit muy - ananee muy — قَنّينة ماي - قَناني ماي |
| | | Section 2, conversations. — القِسم الثّاني، الحِوارات. |
| | | Conversation 1 — الحِوار الأوّل. |
| | | A- 3indak ka3ik? — أ- عِنْدَك كَعِك؟ · B- Eh! — ب- ايْ! |
| | | A- Baddi ka3keh w 3assir. — أ- بَدّي كَعْكة وعَصير. · B- Tfadall. — ب- تْفَضّل. |
| | | A- Shokran. — أ- شُكْراً. · B- Ahlan wa sahlan — ب- أهلاً وسهلاً. |
| | | Conversation 2 — الحِوار الثّاني. |
| | | A- Ya3tik l3afyeh. — أ- يَعْطيك العافْية. · B- Ahlein. — ب- أهْلين. |
| | | A- Baddi man2oushit za3tar. — أ- بَدّي مَنْقوشِة زَعْتَر. · B- Tfadall. — ب- تْفَضّل. |
| | | A- Shokran. — أ- شُكْراً. · B- Ahlan. — ب- أهْلاً. |
| | | Conversation 3 — الحِوار الثّالث. |
| | | A- Mar7aba! — أ- مَرحَبا! · B- Ahlein, tfadall. — ب- أهْلين، تْفَضّل. |
| | | A- 3indak 3assir laymoun? — أ- عِنْدَك عَصير لَيْمون؟ · B- Eh, tfadall. — ب- ايْ، تْفَضّل. |
| | | A- Shokran. — أ- شُكْراً. · B- Ahlan. — ب- أهْلاً. |
| 35 | 2.B | 1- 3indi ktab. — ١- عِندي كِتاب. |
| | | 2- Baddoh finjan ahweh. — ٢- بَدّه فِنْجان قَهْوة. |
| | | 3- Shou baddik? — ٣- شو بَدِّك؟ |
| | | 4- Shou badda? — ٤- شو بَدّا؟ |
| | | 5- Shou badkon? — ٥- شو بَدْكُن؟ |
| | | 6- 3indkon bayt? — ٦- عِنْدْكُن بيت؟ |
| | | 7- 3indi ktabak bass mish ktaba. — ٧- عِندي كِتابَك بَس مِش كِتابا. |
| | | 8- Baddi ahweh bass mish halla2. — ٨- بَدّي قَهْوة بَس مِش هَلّق. |
| | | 9- 3indkon argileh? — ٩- عِنْدْكُن أرْجِيلة؟ |
| | | 10- Badna argileh tiffa7tein. — ١٠- بَدْنا أرْجِيلة تُفّاحْتين. |
| | | 11- 3indik saff halla2? — ١١- عِنْدِك صَفّ هَلّق؟ |
| 36 | 3.B | 1- Hinni 3indon siyarah. — ١- هِنّ عِنْدُن سيّارة. |
| | | 2- Hiyye badda ka3keh. — ٢- هِيّ بَدّا كَعْكة. |
| | | 3- Huwwe 3indoh ktab. — ٣- هُوّ عِنْدُه كِتاب. |
| | | 4- Baddak argileh? — ٤- بَدّك أرْجِيلة؟ |

# ANSWERS

| Page | Exercise | 7ad | Wein? | Fow2 | Ta7t | Eddam | Fi |
|------|----------|-----|-------|------|------|-------|-----|
| 38 | 1.C | حَدا | وِين؟ | فَوق | تَحت | قُدّام | في + فيّ |
| | | حَدّي | وِينّي | فَوقي | تَحتي | قُدّامي | فيكي |
| | | حَدّك | وِينَك | فَوقَك | تَحتَك | قُدّامَك | فيه |
| | | حَدّه | وِينه | فَوقه | تَحته | قُدّامه | فيها |
| | | حَدّنا | وِينا | فَوقنا | تَحتنا | قُدّامنا | فينا |
| | | حَدّكُن | وِينكُن | فَوقكُن | تَحتكُن | قُدّامكُن | فيكُن |
| | | حَدّهُن | وِينهُن | فَوقهُن | تَحتهُن | قُدّامهُن | فيهُن |

### 39  2.C

1- Bi — ـ بـ
2- 7ad / fow2 / bi — حدا / فوق / بـ
3- Bi — ـ بـ
4- 3a — ـ
5- Ta7t — تحت
6- Wara / Ta7t — ورا / تحت

### 40  3.C

| | |
|---|---|
| Bsayneh = cat | بسينة |
| Kalib = dog | كلب |
| Feel = elephant | فيل |
| 7ayyeh = snake | حيّة |
| Farah = mouse | فارة |
| Shajrah = tree | شجرة |

Wein libsayneh? — وين البسينة؟ — Libsayneh 7ad lkalib.
Wein l7ayyeh? — وين الحيّة؟ — L7ayyeh eddam lfeel.
Wein Zizi? — وين زيزي؟ — Zizi bisiyarah.
Wein ljibneh? — وين الجبنة؟ — Ljibneh wara lfarah.
Wein Karim? — وين كريم؟ — Karim bilmat3am
Wein lkalib? — وين الكلب؟ — Lkalib 3alkanabayeh.
Wein siyarah? — وين السيّارة؟ — Siyarah ta7t shajrah.

### 41  4.C

Picture one — الصورة الأولى
Libsayneh 3ashajrah. — البسينة على الشجرة.
Shantah ta7t shajrah. — الشنتة تحت الشجرة.
Shantah 3al2arid. — الشنتة على الأرض.
Picture two — الصورة الثانية
Libsayneh ta7t shajrah. — البسينة تحت الشجرة.
Shantah fow2 libsayneh. — الشنتة فوق البسينة.
Shantah bishajrah. — الشنتة بالشجرة.

# Answers

| Page | Exercise | | |
|---|---|---|---|

**Picture three**

| Shantah eddam libsayneh. | الشنطة قدام اللبسينة. |
|---|---|
| Libsayneh wara/ 7ad shantah. | اللبسينة ورا / حد الشنطة. |
| Shajrah 7ad libsayneh w shantah. | الشجرة حد اللبسينة والشنطة. |

**42  5.C**

| Q- 3indik bayt? | A- Eh, bil7amra. | سن عندك بيت؟ — آه، بالحمرا. |
|---|---|---|
| Q- Wein kibbayti? | A- 3atawleh. | سن وين كبايتي؟ — عالطاولة. |
| Q- 3inda siyarah? | A- Eh, ta7t shoghlah, bilmaw2af. | سن عندا سيارة؟ — آه، تحت شغلا، بالموقف. |
| Q- Wein m3almitna? | A- Hiyye bisaff eddamna. | سن وين معلمتنا؟ — هي بالصف قدامنا. |
| Q- Wein shanttoh? | A- 3atawleh warak. | سن وين شنطه؟ — عالطاولة ورك. |
| Q- Wein maktabik? | A- 7ad maktaboh. | سن وين مكتبك؟ — حد مكتبه. |

**45  1.D**

| Taxi conversation. | | الحوار مع التاكسي. |
|---|---|---|
| You: 3al7amra? | Driver: eh, tfadall. | إنت: عالحمرا؟ — الشوفير: أي، تفضل. |
| You: ya3tik l3afyeh. | Driver: allah y3afik, ahlein. | إنت: يعطيك العافية. — الشوفير: الله يعافيك، أهلين. |
| You: binzal hown 3mol ma3rouf. Tfadall. | Driver: yisslamou, ma3 salameh. | إنت: بنزل هون عمول معروف، تفضل. — الشوفير: بسلمو مع السلامة. |
| You: allah yssalmak. | | إنت: الله يسلمك. |

| Restaurant conversation. | | الحوار بالمطعم. |
|---|---|---|
| You: ya3tik l3afyeh. | Waiter: ahlein, tfadall. | إنت: يعطيك العافية. — الغارسون: أهلين تفضل. |
| You: baddi anninet muy iza bitreed. | Waiter: tikram isstaz. | إنت: بدي قنينة ماي إذا بتريد. — الغارسون: تكرم أستاذ. |
| You: 3mol ma3rouf li7ssab? | Waiter: tikram , tfadall. | إنت: عمول معروف الحساب؟ — الغارسون: تكرم تفضل. |
| You: yisslamou, killak zow2. | Waiter: ahlan, ma3 salameh. | إنت: بسلمو كلك ذوق. — الغارسون: أهلا مع السلامة. |

**48  1.A**

| Bya3rif = C | بيعرف — C= |
|---|---|
| Byit3allam = B | بيتعلم — B= |
| Mni7ki = A | منحكي — A= |
| Byishtighlou = D | بيشتغلو — D= |

**48  2.A**

| | | | | Pronoun |
|---|---|---|---|---|
| بَعْمَل | بَحْكي | بَعْرِف | | أنا |
| بْيَعْمَل | بْيِحْكي | بِيعْرِف | | هو |
| مْنَعْمَل | مْنِحْكي | مْنِعْرِف | | نحنا |
| بْتَعْمَلو | بْتِحْكو | بْتِعْرْفو | | إنتو |
| بْتَعْمَل | بْتِحْكي | بْتِعْرِف | | هي |
| بْتَعْمَل | بْتِحْكي | بْتِعْرِف | | إنت |
| بْيَعْمَلو | بْيِحْكو | بْيِعْرْفو | | هن |
| بْيَعْمَلي | بْيِحْكي | بْيِعْرْفي | | إنت |

**49  1.B**

| نحنا بدنا نعمل اجتماع: |
|---|
| إنت بتك تعرفي شو وإسمك؟ |

**50  1.C**

| الشب بيعقل اكبر. |
|---|

# ANSWERS

| Page | Exercise | | |
|---|---|---|---|

هو بيشتغل عالكمبيوتر

الطالب بيشتغل بالمدرسة.

الشركة فيها بيحكي فرنسي

1- سارة بتشتغل موظفة بشركة وكمان هي بتتعلّم بلـ AUB.

2- جميل شبب بيشتغل اكل بمطعم خبراً.

3- جاد وكارلو بيشتغلو دكانة

4- جورج وكارلا ما فيهن بيشتغلو هلّ عشان هنّ بالجامعة بس بدّن يتعلّمو ويحكو عربي

**52   2.C**

**52   3.C** — Ahmad    Nariman    Karim

بيشتغلو    بيتعلّمو

بيشتغل    بيتعلّم

**53   4.C**

|  |  |  |
|---|---|---|
| To watch (I watch) | 7idir (ana bi7dar) | حضر (أنا بحضر) |
| To study (I study) | Darass (ana bidross) | درس (أنا بدرس) |
| To come (I come) | Ija (ana biji) | إجى (أنا بجي) |

أنا — بدي إحضر فيلم.

هنّ — بدّن يحضرو فيلم.

إنتِ — بدّك تحضري فيلم.

هو — بدو يحضر فيلم.

إنتو — بدكن تحضرو فيلم.

نحنا — بدنا نحضر فيلم.

هي — بدا تحضر فيلم.

إنت — بدّك تحضر فيلم.

أنا — بدي إحضر عربي.

هنّ — بدّن يدرسو عربي.

إنتِ — بدّك تدرسي عربي.

هو — بدو يدرس عربي.

إنتو — بدكن تدرسو عربي.

نحنا — بدنا ندرس عربي.

هي — بدا تدرس عربي.

إنت — بدّك تدرس عربي.

أنا — بدي إجي عالصف.

هنّ — بدّن يجو عالصف.

إنتِ — بدّك تجي عالصف.

هو — بدو يجي عالصف.

إنتو — بدكن تجو عالصف.

نحنا — بدنا نجي عالصف.

هي — بدا تجي عالصف.

إنت — بدّك تجي عالصف.

**55   1.A** — >>>>>>>>>>>>>>>>>>>>>>>>

**56   2.A**

|  |  |
|---|---|
| My number is .... | رقمي سبعة صفر سبعة ثلاثة سبعة أربعة واحد سبعة |
| (Name of friend)'s number is... | رقم (اسم رفيقك) صفر ثلاثة ثمانية خمسة |
| (Name of friend)'s number is... | رقم (اسم رفيقك) صفر واحد عشرة ثمانية خمسة |

**56   3.A**

|  |  |
|---|---|
| Khamsseh sab3ah tnein. | خمسة سبعة تنين |
| Sitteh tiss3ah tnein sab3ah tnein. | ستة تسعة تنين سبعة تنين |

**58   1.B**

|  |  |
|---|---|
| From right to left. | من اليمين للشمال |
| Tilit kibbayeh. | تلت كبّاية |
| Robo3 kibbayeh. | ربع كبّاية |
| Noss kibbayeh. | نص كبّاية |
| Ta2riban robo3 kibbayeh. | تقريباً ربع كبّاية |
| Ta2riban noss kibbayeh. | تقريباً نص كبّاية |

**58   2.B**

أنا بشتغل من الساعة ثمانية لثمانية خمسة.

بحضر تلفزيون الساعة نمانة نصف.

بنام تقريباً عالساعة سبعة وعشر.

يحكي طيش نحن من الساعة العربي الساعة ...

Number puzzle grid (answer)

وكيف بيقضّوا بالجمعل جد مطعم مروش... نحبي من شغل بتحضر تلفزيون وبذرس شوفي هي كان بدا تشتغل مديرة المدرسة بس عندا شغل كبير منيح؟